ROBINSON'S PARADIGMS
AND EXERCISES IN
SYRIAC GRAMMAR

ROBINSON'S PARADIGMS AND EXERCISES IN
SYRIAC GRAMMAR

FIFTH EDITION

REVISED BY
J. F. COAKLEY

OXFORD
UNIVERSITY PRESS

OXFORD
UNIVERSITY PRESS

Great Clarendon Street, Oxford OX2 6DP

Oxford University Press is a department of the University of Oxford.
It furthers the University's objective of excellence in research, scholarship,
and education by publishing worldwide in

Oxford New York

Auckland Cape Town Dar es Salaam Hong Kong Karachi Kuala Lumpur
Madrid Melbourne Mexico City Nairobi New Delhi Shanghai Taipei Toronto

With offices in

Argentina Austria Brazil Chile Czech Republic France Greece
Guatemala Hungary Italy Japan South Korea Poland Portugal
Singapore Switzerland Thailand Turkey Ukraine Vietnam

Oxford is a registered trade mark of Oxford University Press
in the UK and in certain other countries

Published in the United States
by Oxford University Press Inc., New York

First edition 1915
Second edition 1939
Third edition 1949
Fourth edition 1962
First published as paperback 1981

British Library Cataloguing in Publication Data
Data available

Library of Congress Cataloging in Publication Data
Data applied for
ISBN 0-19-925409-5
ISBN 0-19-926129-6 (pbk.)

3 5 7 9 10 8 6 4

Printed in Great Britain
on acid-free paper by
Biddles Ltd., King's Lynn, Norfolk

PREFACE TO THE FIFTH EDITION

T. H. Robinson's *Paradigms and Exercises in Syriac Grammar* was first published in 1915, and the text was very little changed through the fourth edition of 1962 revised by L. H. Brockington. Yet although it was tried and found serviceable by generations of students, the book had some unsatisfactory features and it was generally acknowledged to be in need of a thorough revision. That is what I have attempted in this new edition. The basic structure of the lessons remains, but their rhythm has been slightly altered, and, in particular, verbs now appear at an earlier point. Much of the explanatory text, and many of the sentences for translation, are new. I have, however, tried to avoid introducing too many refinements into the grammar, which, it seemed to me, would defeat the purpose of Robinson's book to be a simple and friendly introduction to the language. A student who, while learning from Robinson, wants to refer to a more comprehensive treatment of the subject, can be recommended to consult T. Nöldeke's *Compendious Syriac Grammar* (2nd edn. 1898; English translation 1904), which is still the most authoritative work; or L. Costaz, *Grammaire syriaque* (Beirut, 2nd edn. 1964), which is more concise and is well indexed.

J.F. COAKLEY

May 2002

CONTENTS

1 . INTRODUCTION

The name 'Syriac' comes into English from the word used
by classical Syriac writers to denote their community and
language, *Suryaya* (ܣܘܪܝܝܐ). This word had, it seems,
nothing to do with the Roman province of Syria on the
Mediterranean coast,[1] and in fact it was further east, in
Edessa, in Mesopotamia, that Syriac emerged as a literary
language, starting in the first century CE.

Syriac is a dialect of the Aramaic language, which in turn
belongs to the Semitic family of languages. Aramaic was an
international language during the time of the Achaemenid
Persian empire of the sixth to fourth centuries BCE; but by
the time that Syriac emerged, this empire had broken up,
and Aramaic subsisted only in various local dialects. Tech-
nically, Syriac is one of the 'Eastern' group of these dialects,
along with the Aramaic of the Babylonian Talmud, and
Mandaic. The Aramaic of Palestine, hypothetically the language of Jesus and represented in writing by (for example)
some of the Dead Sea Scrolls, belongs to the 'Western'
group of dialects, and is therefore a slightly more distant

---

[1] Historically, *Suryaya* has often come into English as 'Syrian'
rather than 'Syriac', not only as a noun (as in 'St. Ephrem the
Syrian') but also as an adjective (as in 'Syrian Orthodox Church').
The result has been a more or less incorrect association with
'Syria'. The student will usually have to explain to non-specialist
friends that Syriac is not the language of the modern country of
Syria (which is, of course, Arabic).

relative of Syriac.[2] Hebrew, a sister language of Aramaic, is
more distant yet, although it belongs to the same subfamily
usually known as 'Northwest Semitic'. The other major
Semitic languages – Arabic, Ethiopic and ancient Akkadian
– are further away linguistically, although between Syriac
and Arabic there are close historical connections. After the
rise of Islam Arabic became the second, and later the first,
language of many Syriac-speakers, and they sometimes
wrote Arabic using the Syriac script. The pronunciation of
the two languages also interacted.

The place of Syriac in Semitic linguistics is one reason for
studying the language; but there are other and, in fact,
more usual ones. In Western biblical scholarship, Syriac has
been an important subject since the Renaissance, and many
students come to it on account of the ancient Syriac
versions of the Old and New Testaments and the tradition
of commentary writing. Other students, if not the majority,
want to read the works of native Syriac writers of poetry,
history, and theology. Still other students have an interest
in one or another of the living Syriac churches and their
tradition and liturgy. This book attempts to serve those who
want to learn the language for any of these kinds of reasons.

In ancient times the Syriac language-area overlapped the
Roman and Persian empires. Later, this geo-political division was broadly reinforced by ecclesiastical boundaries, so
that the Syriac-speaking communities in the two empires

---

[2] It is sometimes heard that Syriac is the language of Jesus. That
is so only in the sense that both are Aramaic.

were more or less isolated from each other. The result was two grammatical traditions, or sub-dialects, within the language, the West Syriac and East Syriac.[3] The Syriac script too developed differently away from its oldest form in these two traditions. For reasons of good pedagogy an introductory grammar must choose East or West. In this book the West Syriac tradition will be followed, although with some exceptions (to do with pronunciation, on which see §3 below). An introduction to reading in the other scripts is given in Appendices B and C.

[3] In older literature, often 'Jacobite' (West) and 'Nestorian' (East); but these names are best avoided.

2. THE SCRIPT

Syriac is written with an alphabet of twenty-two letters, which is the same, in its underlying form, as that used by other Aramaic dialects and by Hebrew. Syriac uses a distinctive script to write this alphabet. Of the Syriac script there are three main varieties (also usually called 'scripts'), corresponding to the different traditions mentioned in §1. This lesson deals with reading and writing the West Syriac script, also known as *serṭa* or *serṭo*.

The script is written from right to left, and it is cursive: that is, words are written without lifting the pen between every letter, and the letters can take two, or four, different forms depending on their place in a word and the letters around them. The table opposite shows the letters in each form, with the corresponding Hebrew in the last column. The 'transliteration' roughly indicates pronunciation; but on this see the next lesson.

It will be observed that all the letters can connect to a preceding letter (that is, from the right), but that the letters ، ܡ ܘ ܝ ܖ ܠ do not connect to a following letter (to the left).

The combination *lamad-alaph* is written ܠܐ (or ܠܐ- when connected to a preceding letter). Sometimes (although not in this book) the combination *alaph-lamad* is written -ܐܠ.

A curved form of *alaph* (ܵ) is used in this book at the beginnings of words, but the straight form (ܐ) is also correct in all positions.

name[1]	translit-eration	alone	joined to another letter on left	on both sides	on right	Hebrew
alaph	ʾ	‍ or ⁄			‍	א
beth	b	‍	‍	‍	‍	ב
gamal	g	‍	‍	‍	‍	ג
dalath	d	?			?	ד
he	h	‍			‍	ה
waw	w	‍			‍	ו
zayn	z	‍			‍	ז
ḥeth	ḥ	‍	‍	‍	‍	ח
ṭeth	ṭ	‍	‍	‍	‍	ט
yod	y	‍	‍	‍	‍	י
kaph	k	‍	‍	‍	‍	כ
lamad	l	‍	‍	‍	‍	ל
mem	m	‍	‍	‍	‍	מ
nun	n	‍	‍	‍	‍	נ
semkath	s	‍	‍	‍	‍	ס
ʿe	ʿ	‍	‍	‍	‍	ע
pe	p	‍	‍	‍	‍	פ
ṣade	ṣ	‍			‍	צ
qoph	q	‍	‍	‍	‍	ק
resh	r	‍			‍	ר
shin	š	‍	‍	‍	‍	ש
taw	t	‍			‍	ת

[1] The names of the letters are spelled conventionally. For the correct Syriac forms see the headings in the Syriac-English glossary.

The following are models and hints for writing each letter.

Alaph always ends in a down-stroke (not as in Arabic), which extends slightly below the line.

Beth is wider and flatter on top than *kaph*.

Gamal is almost all below the line and it extends back below a preceding letter.

Dalath always has a dot below. Cf. *resh*.

He is the same height as *beth*.

Waw differs from *qoph* in that it never connects on the left.

Zayn is like *alaph* but shorter, only as high as *beth*. There is no curved form.

Ḥeth has two spikes. It is shorter than *beth*, but ideally a little taller than *yod*.

Ṭeth. The loop goes below the line.

Yod is a single spike, shorter than *nun*.

Kaph is narrower and rounder than *beth*. The tail of the final form bends to the left.

Lamad is the same height as *alaph* and must be clearly taller than ʿe. Some teachers say to aim for an angle of 45°. When it is at the end of a word, the finishing stroke goes up in parallel.

Lamad-alaph. The *lamad* loses its slant. When it is not connected from the right, the *lamad* begins on a down-stroke.

Mem. The tail of the final form is turned down.

Nun has exactly the height of *beth* or *he* and must be made clearly taller than *yod*. The final form extends below a preceding letter.

Semkath. Ideally the left loop should be slightly higher than the right.

ʿE is like *lamad* but shorter. Its slant distinguishes it from *nun*.

Pe is taller than *beth* but not as tall as *alaph*.

Ṣade has a very small spike, and a large hook below the line.

Qoph always has a finishing stroke to the left, whether it connects to a following letter or not.

Resh always has a dot above. Cf. *dalath*.

Shin. Aim for a triangular shape, bringing the pen back to fill it in. It must be larger and bolder than *yod*. A rounder shape (like ▲)is also acceptable.

Taw finishes with a rightward stroke.

Diacritical points. Syriac is correctly written with a variety of diacritical points intended to distinguish homographs (different words that are spelled alike, for example, ܐܲܝܕܵܐ/ *ayda* 'which' and ܐܝܼܕܵܐ/ *ida* 'hand'). These points are generally redundant when pronunciation is specified by vowel-signs, as it will be in this book, and they will be omitted in the lessons to follow. (Before reading an unvocalized text, see further on diacritical points in Appendix B.)

There are, however, two particular diacritical marks which will be printed here and should always be written. One of these is the pair of points known as *seyame* ('things placed') that indicates the plural of nouns, most adjectives, and some verb forms. For example, 'king' is written ܡܲܠܟܵܐ and 'kings' ܡܲܠܟܹ̈ܐ. *Seyame* may go anywhere on a word, but when writing, it is best to put it near the middle, and over a short letter if possible. The letter *resh* (ܪ) often attracts the *seyame*, which then replaces its dot; thus ܦܹ̈ܐܪܵܐ / ܦܹܐܪܵܐ 'fruit/fruits'. The other obligatory diacritical mark is the dot over ܗ in certain pronoun suffixes indicating the feminine. (For these see §§6, 18.)

Punctuation. The practice of copyists has always varied. In this book, we follow a system usual among editors. The full point ends a sentence, as in English, and the various double points ⁖ : ؛ represent divisions within a sentence. There is no question mark.[2] A more major division in the text is shown by four points ❖ .

---

[2] At least in old manuscripts; but modern writers and editors sometimes use 'ؤ'.

Abbreviations may be indicated by a line over the beginning of the word, e.g. ܫܘܒ = ܫܘܒܚܐ 'glory'; ܘܫܡ = ܘܫܪܟܐ 'etc.'. Sometimes the same line indicates that letters are to be read as numbers (see pp. 136-7); e.g. ܫܝܛ = 319.

Exercises

Write in transliteration, using the English letters in the table on p. 5.[3]

لحقصيرا /مبع /حزمو افزما قوملوهه مزيمر ملعوت موسل

هووزما /ليهوما /قصمممرا /وسليلم ، مجعم محلا فموا هوريلا

Write in Syriac characters:

ṣly wrdyn ʿlyh ywmtʾ mdyntʾ šlmyn klbʾ ʿlyhwn
klmdm mtqrʾ ʿmṣw lḥddʾ mṭl mstkl šḥlp lʾ thwʾ ṭlytʾ
sbr ydʿ ydʿtwn mlk mlkʾ ḥlpwhy nbyʾ ʿm ʿmmʾ mlʾkʾ
wʾzl dyrʾ rdʾ qṭl gbrʾ ttplḥ ʾrkwn ʾnšʾ ʾnttʾ msybrnwtʾ

---

[3] Some of these words reappear with vowels in the exercise to §3.

3 . PRONUNCIATION

This lesson deals with the pronunciation of consonants and
vowels, and how this pronunciation is indicated by the
writing system.[1]

Consonants. The letters transliterated as *z l m n s r,* and *h*
w y when used as consonants, may be pronounced as in
English. The others are as follows.

ܐ is a glottal stop; but more often it is quiescent: see p.
14 below.

ܚ corresponds to Arabic ح, a stronger *h* than ܗ. Many
students, not strictly correctly, pronounce it like *ch* in
German *ich* (as in Hebrew).

ܛ corresponds to Arabic ط, an emphatic *t*. Most
English-speakers do not distinguish it in pronunciation
from ܬ.

ܥ corresponds to Arabic ع, a stop far back in the throat,
like a gagging sound. Some students succeed in
making this sound; some make it a simple glottal stop
like ܐ.

ܨ corresponds to Arabic ص, an emphatic *s*. The pronunciation *ts*, borrowed from Hebrew, is conventional.

ܩ corresponds to Arabic ق and is a sound further back in

---

[1] In this lesson and occasionally in later ones, Syriac is written in
English letters. This is simply to help with pronunciation, and
there is no attempt at a consistent or scientific system.

the throat than ܩ. It is worthwhile, to avoid misspelling errors later, to try to make this sound distinctive.

ܫ is pronounced *sh* (*š*).

The letters ܬ ܓ ܕ ܟ ܦ ܒ (bgdkpt, pronounced *begadkefath*) have two alternative pronunciations: 'stopped' (hard) and 'spirantized' (soft). When spirantized,

  ܒ (*b*) becomes *v*.

  ܓ (*g*) becomes like Arabic غ, something like French *r*. Not all students attempt to make this sound.

  ܕ (*d*) becomes voiced *th*, as in *there*.

  ܟ (*k*) becomes like Arabic خ, that is, like *ch* in German *acht*. Note that this approaches the usual pronunciation of ܟ.

  ܦ (*p*) becomes *f*.

  ܬ (*t*) becomes unvoiced *th*, as in *thin*.

(In transliteration, the spirantized letters are often shown with underlines: b̲ g̲ d̲ k̲ p̲ t̲.) In some manuscripts and printed books, especially the Bible, the hard and soft pronunciations are indicated by dots: a dot above the letter, known as *qushaya* ('hard'), or below, *rukaka* ('soft').[2] Thus, ܒ is pronounced *b* and ܒ is pronounced *v*, etc. (Notice that ܕ must be *dalath* with *qushaya*, not *resh*.)

Generally, a *bgdkpt* letter is spirantized after a vowel, and otherwise pronounced hard. Most of the time this rule is

---

[2] Properly, *quššāyā* (ܩܘܫܝܐ) and *rukkākā* (ܪܘܟܟܐ). To distinguish these dots from other diacritical points they are sometimes written in red in manuscripts. In print they should ideally be smaller.

easy to apply, but sometimes it is not. An indistinct vowel (in Hebrew, vocal *shewa*) before a *bgdkpt* letter will cause it to be spirantized, and a letter that is doubled is always pronounced hard. Syriac does not show either of these things in the writing system and, unless the text actually uses *qushaya* and *rukaka* points, the reader has to decide on pronunciation from knowledge of grammar and some supplementary rules. To avoid overloading the present lesson these rules are set out in Appendix A, and they should become familiar by experience. In this book, *qushaya* and *rukaka* are supplied when the pronunciation is unexpected or might be in doubt, at least on the first occurrence of a word and in the Syriac-English glossary.

Vowels. Anciently, some vowels became part of the spelling of words, using the letters *waw* (for *o* and *u*), *yod* (for *i* and *e*), *alaph* (for *a*, *ā*, *e*, *i*) and *he* (for *a* and *e*). For example:

| ܡܘܫܐ | *Muše* | ܗܠܝܢ | *hālen* | ܛܘܒ | *tuḇ* |
| ܣܝܡ | *sim* | ܟܐܦܐ | *kip̄ā* | ܟܬܒܗ | *ktāḇeh.* |

Later, a system of vowel-signs was superimposed; or rather, each of the two traditions of pronunication, East and West, developed its own system of vowel-signs. The West Syriac vowel-signs, based on Greek letters, are ˈ ˊ ˃ ˒ ˓ . In this book we use these signs, although, following the custom of scholarly Syriac, we depart from the West Syriac tradition of pronunciation in two places, in order to preserve a more original phonology.[3] First: the sign ' will indicate *ā* (as in *father*).[4] Second: we will distinguish an additional vowel *o* and indicate it by a dot above the letter *waw* in place of the vowel-sign ʿ. Thus we have the following:

sign[5]	value	used alone	with vowel letters	value
'	*ā*	ܕ	ܟܐ, ܟܗ	*bā*
ˊ	*a*	ܕ		*ba*
ˋ	*e*	ܕ	ܟܗ , ܟܐ , ܟܕ	*be*
ˏ	*i*	ܕ	ܟܐ (or ܟܝ), ܟܕ	*bi*
ˎ	*u*		ܟܘ	*bu*
·	*o*		ܟܘ	*bo*.

Vowel letters are always used when the vowel is *o*, and almost always when it is *u*. (The common words ܟܠ *kul* 'every' and ܡܛܠ *meṭul* 'because' are exceptional in not being spelled with ܘ.[6]) Likewise, the sign ˊ does not very often appear without *yod* or *alaph*. As shown above, *waw* attracts the vowel-sign over itself, and *yod* may also do this. Otherwise, the sign is written on the preceding consonant. The vowel-signs (but not usually ˊ) may go upside down below the letters if there is not room above; thus ܒ ܒ ܒ ܒ.

---

[3] Both these points are, in fact, features of the East Syriac vowel system. For other differences in this system, see Appendix C.

[4] That is, rather than *o*, the West Syriac pronunciation. So we transliterate ܟܬܒܐ as *ktābā*, not *ktobo*.

[5] By name the signs are: ' *zkāpā*; ˊ *ptāḥā*; ˋ *rbāṣā*; ˏ *ḥbāṣā*; ˎ *ʿāṣā*. (These names will not be used again in this book.)

[6] More correctly, these are *kol* and *meṭol*, but the *o* vowel cannot be shown when the *waw* is not written, and the West Syriac pronunciations with *u* are conventional.

Occasionally it is useful to make the distinction between 'long' and 'short' vowels. The vowel ˊ is always long; ˊ, ˋ and ˊo are usually long; ˋ may be long (and is always so when spelled - ـˋ-) or short. The vowel ˋ is always short.

Alaph and *yod*. After another consonant *alaph* is usually 'quiescent'; that is, it simply carries the vowel of that consonant, as in ܟܐܦܐ *kipa* 'stone'. *Alaph* can also have its own vowel (and it must do so at the beginning of a word), as in ܐܟܠ *ʾākel* 'eats'. But if it is preceded by a vowelless consonant, its vowel moves over onto that consonant, as in ܕܐܟܠ *dākel* (from *d-ʾākel*) 'who eats'. *Yod* is somewhat the same. If it would be without a full vowel at the beginning of a syllable, it assumes the vowel *i*, as in ܝܗܘܕܝܐ *ihuḏāye* 'Jews'. These rules for *alaph* and *yod* will be frequently referred to in the grammar to come.

Silent letters. Occasionally spelling does not follow pronunciation exactly. In a text with vowel-signs, a consonant that is silent may be indicated by *linea occultans*, a short line (lit., 'hiding line') written under the letter, for example in ܡܕܝܢܬܐ *mḏitā* (not *mḏintā*), ܢܐܫܐ *nāšā*, ܐܙܐ *āzā*. In suffixes and in a few common words, silent letters are not always marked at all, e.g. ܐܝܟ *ak* (not *ayk*) 'as'.

The words from p. 12, supplied with vowel-signs, are:

ܡܘܫܐ	*Muše*	ܗܠܝܢ	*hālen*	ܬܘܒ	*tub*
ܣܝܡ	*sim*	ܟܐܦܐ	*kipā*	ܟܬܒܗ	*ktābeh*.

The following are further examples of words vocalized, with their pronunciation:

ܡܠܟܐ	*malkā*	ܘܪܕܐ	*wardā*	ܝܪܚܐ	*yarḥā*

ܪܸܫܹܐ *riše*   ܠܶܘܿܐ *hwāṯ* (or *h'wāṯ*)   ܘܵܘ *waw*

ܡܸܡܲܠܵܠܘ *m'malālu*   ܐܘܼܪܚܵܬ݂ܵܐ *urḥāṯā*   ܕܲܗܒ݂ܵܐ *dahḇā*.

Exercises

Read the following words aloud. (They are proper names
or other terms that might be recognizable.)

Write the following words in Syriac characters, with vowel-
signs and with *rukaka* and *qushaya*. You may assume here
that *i* and *ei* are to be written with *yod*, and *o* and *u* with
waw; and that words ending in -*ā* end in *alaph* in Syriac.

šmayā	*hwāṯ*	*'eṯḥzi*	*rišānā*	*šubḥā*	*galyaṯ*
hālein	*'amirā*	*ṭubān*	*'aḇdā*	*l'aylein*	*nmalel*
sā'em	*šliḥā*	*ṣawmā*	*'aḥay*	*'āmrin*	*parṣopā*
'damā	*sāymin*	*sagi'ā*	*hayment*	*ṣbuṯā*	*'lawhy*
	qdāmaykon	*malpānuṯā*	*mmalālu*	*peṯgāmā*.	

4. PRONOUNS . PARTICLES . SIMPLE SENTENCES

Pronouns are of four kinds: personal, demonstrative, inter-rogative, and relative. The *personal pronouns* are as follows:

person	singular		plural	
1st	ܐܷܢܳܐ	I	ܚܢܰܢ	we
2nd masculine	ܐܰܢ݉ܬ	you (*m.*)	ܐܰܢ݉ܬܘܿܢ	you (*m.*)
2nd feminine	ܐܰܢ݉ܬܝ	you (*f.*)	ܐܰܢ݉ܬܷܝܢ	you (*f.*)
3rd masculine	ܗܘ	he	ܗܷܢܘܿܢ	they (*m.*)
3rd feminine	ܗܝ	she	ܗܷܢܷܝܢ	they (*f.*).

For the 1st person pl. there is a longer and less common form ܐܰܢܰܚܢܰܢ (*naḥnan*). Note also the silent letters in ܐܰܢ݉ܬ and ܐܰܢ݉ܬܝ (both pronounced *at*), ܐܰܢ݉ܬܘܿܢ (*aton*) and ܐܰܢ݉ܬܷܝܢ (*aten*).

A personal pronoun may be used to make a simple A-is-B sentence, e.g.

ܐܰܢ݉ܬ ܡܰܠܟܳܐ.   You are king.

In such sentences, the 1st- and 3rd-person pronouns have shorter, so-called enclitic, forms:

	sing.	pl.
1st	ܐ݈ܢܳܐ	ܚܢܰܢ
3rd masc.	ܝܘ	ܐܷܢܘܿܢ
3rd fem.	ܝܗ	ܐܷܢܷܝܢ

The 3rd sing. forms are shown with no vowel. If they follow a word ending in a vowel, they form a diphthong with *-w* or *-y*. Thus we have ܡܰܠܟ݈ܬ݂ܳܝ (*malkṯāy*) 'She is queen'. In the masculine, the diphthong *-āw* becomes *-aw*, giving ܡܰܠܟܰܘ (not ܡܰܠܟܳܘ) *malkaw* 'he is king'. Following a consonant,

these enclitics become ܗ݂ܘ and ܝ݂ܗ , for example after ܡܢ
('who?') giving ܡܢ ܗ݂ܘ and ܡܢ ܝ݂ܗ 'who is he/she?' The combination ܗ݂ܘ ܘ݁ becomes ܗ݂ܘܝܘ 'he is' or 'it is he'.

The *demonstrative pronouns* are as follows:

	sing.		pl.	
	masc.	fem.	masc.	fem.
this, these	ܗܢܐ	ܗܕܐ	ܗܠܝܢ	
that, those	ܗܘ	ܗܝ	ܗܢܘܢ	ܗܢܝܢ

There are also shorter forms ܢܐ (for ܗܢܐ) and ܕܐ (for ܗܕܐ), less
commonly seen. With the enclitic pronoun, ܗܢܐ becomes ܗܢܘ,
and ܗܕܐ becomes ܗܕܐ ܗܝ , both meaning 'this is'. The demonstratives can also be adjectives, coming before or after the
noun, as in ܗܢܐ ܓܒܪܐ 'this man', ܗܢܝܢ ܢܫܐ 'those women'.

The *interrogative pronouns* are most usually:

ܡܢ who? ܡܢܐ what?

The combination with the 3rd-person masculine enclitics is
generally written as a single word: ܡܢܘ (for ܡܢ ܗ݂ܘ) 'who is ?'
and ܡܢܘ (for ܡܢܐ ܘ݁) 'what is ?'. With the feminine there is
no contraction, e.g.

ܡܢܐ ܗܝ ܗܕܐ What is this?

Other words for 'what?' are ܡܐ (not to be confused with ܡܢ)
and ܡܐ.

Another set of interrogative pronouns is:

ܐܝܢܐ (*m.*) ܐܝܕܐ (*f.*) ܐܝܠܝܢ (*pl.*) which?

as in ܐܝܕܐ ܗܝ ܗܕܐ which one is this (*f.*)?

ܒܐܝܢܐ ܠܫܢܐ in which language?

also relative pron.
cf p25, n.7

Syriac has four *inseparable particles*, so called because they are written as prefixes to the following word.

    ܒ in, with   ܕ of

    ܘ and   ܠ to, for.

When prefixed to a word, if the following letter has a vowel, then the particle is attached without any vowel, e.g.

$$\text{ܕ-} + \text{ܡܰܠܟܳܐ} = \text{ܕܡܰܠܟܳܐ} \quad \text{of the king.}$$

If the letter has no vowel, the particle takes the vowel *a*:

$$\text{ܒ-} + \text{ܡܕܺܝܢ̱ܬܳܐ} = \text{ܒܰܡܕܺܝܢ̱ܬܳܐ} \quad \text{in the city .}$$

The same rule applies if another particle is then attached: ܘܕܡܰܠܟܳܐ 'and of the king', ܘܒܰܡܕܺܝܢ̱ܬܳܐ 'and in the city'. If the first letter of the word is *alaph*, the vowel moves onto the particle, e.g.

$$\text{ܕ-} + \text{ܐܰܠܳܗܳܐ} = \text{ܕܰܐܠܳܗܳܐ} \quad \text{of God .}$$

The same thing happens with a word beginning with ـܝ :

$$\text{ܕ-} + \text{ܝܺܕܰܥ} = \text{ܕܺܝܺܕܰܥ} \quad \text{who knew .}$$

The particle ـܕ , besides expressing the genitive, functions as the *relative pronoun* ('who', 'which', that'). In this use it combines with the demonstratives ܗܰܘ, ܗܳܝ, ܗܳܢܘܢ, ܗܳܠܶܝܢ and the interrogatives ܐܰܝܠܶܝܢ, ܐܰܝܡܳܐ, ܐܰܝܡܳܐ, as in:

ܐܰܝܠܶܝܢ ܕܒܰܡܕܺܝܢ̱ܬܳܐ   those who are in the city

ܗܰܘ ܕܬܰܠܡܺܝܕܳܐ ܗܘ   the one who is a disciple

ܒܰܪܬܳܐ ܐܰܝܡܳܐ ܕܒܒܰܝܬܳܐ   the daughter who is in the house

ܗܳܝ ܕܡܰܠܟܳܐ ܐܰܢ̱ܬ   the fact that you are king.

More constructions involving ـܕ will appear later in connection with verbs (§8ff.).

In A-is-B sentences using a personal pronoun, the pronoun comes after the predicate, or at least the first word of the predicate. Thus:

ܐܰܢ̱ܬ ܗ̱ܘ ܡܰܠܟܳܐ ܕܺܝܗܽܘ̈ܕܳܝܶܐ   Are you the king of the Jews?

Strictly, the pronoun agrees in person with the logical subject. Thus, there is a difference in meaning between

ܐܰܢ̱ܬܝ ܡܰܠܟܬܳܐ   you are the queen

(which would answer the question 'Who are you?'), and

ܡܰܠܟܬܳܐ ܗ̱ܝ ܐܰܢ̱ܬܝ   the queen is you

(which would answer the question, 'Who is the queen?').
Sometimes, however, this distinction is hard to see, as with
ܐܶܢܳܐ ܐ̱ܢܳܐ / ܐܶܢܳܐ 'It is I' (more usual than ܐܶܢܳܐ ܗܘ). There is little difference between ܕܰܐܠܳܗܳܐ ܒܰܝܬܳܐ ܗܳܢܳܐ and ܗܽܘ ܕܰܐܠܳܗܳܐ ܒܰܝܬܳܐ ܗܳܢܳܐ :
both mean 'This is the house of God.'

Vocabulary

ܡܰܠܟܳܐ	king; *pl.* ܡܰܠ̈ܟܶܐ	ܡܕܺܝܢ̱ܬܳܐ	city
ܡܰܠܟܬܳܐ	queen (*f.*)	ܟܬܳܒܳܐ	book; *pl.* ܟܬܳܒ̈ܶܐ
ܐܰܢ̱ܬ̱ܬܳܐ	woman, wife;	ܦܽܘܩܕܳܢܳܐ	commandments
	pl. ܢܶܫ̈ܶܐ (*f.*)	ܒܰܝܬܳܐ	house (*m.*)
ܓܰܒܪܳܐ	man	ܢܳܡܽܘܣܳܐ	law
ܒܪܳܐ	son	ܥܰܒܕܳܐ	servant; *pl.* ܥܰܒ̈ܕܶܐ
ܒܰܪܬܳܐ	daughter (*f.*)	ܩܽܘܫܬܳܐ	truth
ܐܰܠܳܗܳܐ	God	ܣܽܘܪܝܳܝܳܐ	Syriac
ܡܰܠܦܳܢܳܐ	teacher (*m.*)	ܠܶܫܳܢܳܐ	language
ܡܰܠܦܳܢܺܝܬܳܐ	teacher (*f.*)	ܡܽܘܫܶܐ	Moses

Exercises

Translate into English:

1. *a*. ܓܒܪܐ ܗܘ *b*. ܐܢܬܬܐ ܗܕܐ *c*. ܗܠܝܢ ܦܘܩܕ̈ܢܐ.

2. *a*. ܓܒܪܐ ܗܢܐ *b*. ܗܢܘ ܓܒܪܐ *c*. ܗܢܐ ܓܒܪܐ ܗ̱ܘ.

3. ܥܒܕܐ ܐ̱ܢܐ ܕܡܠܟܬܐ.

4. ܡܢܘ ܗܢܐ. ܗܘܝܘ ܥܒܕܐ ܕܐܠܗܐ.

5. ܗܕܐ ܗ̱ܝ ܡܕܝܢܬܐ ܕܐܠܗܐ.

6. ܐܝܢܐ ܐ̱ܢܐ ܡܠܟܐ ܕܡܕܝܢܬܐ ܗܕܐ.

7. ܗܢܘܢ ܦܘܩܕ̈ܢܐ ܕܢܡܘܣܐ ܐܢ̱ܘܢ.

8. ܐܝܢܐ ܗ̱ܘ ܒܪܐ ܕܡܠܟܬܐ.

9. ܒܪܐ ܘܒܪܬܐ ܕܡܠܟܐ ܐܢ̱ܘܢ.

10. ܗܘܝܘ ܡܠܟܘܬܐ ܕܐܠܗܐ ܡܫܝܚܐ.

11. ܡܢܘ ܐܠܗܐ ܗܘ. ܡܫܝܚܐ ܗ̱ܘ.

Translate into Syriac:

1. these kings; those books; which women? 2. I am the man; you are the king; we are the women. 3. Who are you (*m.*)? Are you the king's servant? 4. She is the wife of the king. 5. They are the servants of the king of the city. 6. These commandments are in the law of Moses. 7. I am a teacher (*f.*) to (*use* ܠ-) the king's daughter. 8. Which one is the Syriac book? It is this one. 9. You (*m.*) are a teacher of the truth. 10. These are, in truth, the commandments of God. 11. What is the language of that city?

5. NOUNS AND ADJECTIVES

Nouns and adjectives are inflected according to gender, number and state. Of these categories, gender (masculine and feminine) and number (singular and plural) correspond to the same features of other languages. The three states (absolute, emphatic, construct) are a feature of Aramaic, and require some explanation.

For nouns, the absolute state is the most basic form, although in Syriac it is used in only a few constructions (see below). Most of the time, including in dictionary entries, a noun is found in the emphatic state,[1] which almost always has an *alaph* (ܐ-), or if feminine *taw-alaph* (ܬܐ-), on the end. In older Aramaic this ending had the sense of a definite article, but that has been lost in Syriac. Thus, ܒܲܝܬܵܐ, a noun in the emphatic state, can mean either 'a house' or 'the house'. The third state, the construct, is a form of the noun that can be used directly before another noun to make a genitive. This state too is relatively little used in Syriac, the genitive being more usually expressed with -ܕ.

For adjectives, both absolute and emphatic states are used: the absolute when an adjective is in the predicate, and the emphatic when it is attributive. Thus, ܛܵܒ ܡܲܠܟܵܐ means 'The king is good', but ܡܲܠܟܵܐ ܛܵܒܵܐ 'a (*or* the) good king'. An

---

[1] But in J. Payne Smith's *Compendious Syriac Dictionary* (Oxford 1903), many (not all) nouns are quoted in the absolute state.

adjective alone in the emphatic state is the same as a noun; for example, ܚܲܣܵܐ 'the Evil One', ܪܲܒܵܐ 'great one – master'.

The normal inflectional endings, attached to both nouns and adjectives, are the following:

	masculine		feminine	
	sing.	pl.	sing.	pl.
absolute	—	ܺܝܢ	ܐ	ܳܢ
emphatic	ܐ	ܶܐ	ܬܐ	ܬܐ
construct	—	ܰܝ	ܬ	ܬ

In the feminine sing. emphatic the ܬ, being a *bgdkpt* letter, is pronounced soft after a vowel but also sometimes after a consonant. For some general rules see Appendix A. It is best to remember individual nouns as they are met.

Attaching the endings to the adjective ܛܳܒ we have:

	masculine		feminine	
	sing.	pl.	sing.	pl.
absolute	ܛܳܒ	ܛܳܒܺܝܢ	ܛܳܒܳܐ	ܛܳܒܳܢ
emphatic	ܛܳܒܳܐ	ܛܳܒܶܐ	ܛܳܒܬܐ	ܛܳܒܳܬܐ
construct	ܛܳܒ	ܛܳܒܰܝ	ܛܳܒܰܬ	ܛܳܒܳܬ

Notice that the plural forms of adjectives all take *seyame* except the masculine absolute.

Examples of nouns – here, ܡܰܠܟܳܐ *m.*, and ܟܢܘܫܬܐ *f.* ('synagogue') – in all three states are:

	masculine		feminine	
	sing.	pl.	sing.	pl.
absolute	ܡܠܟ	ܡܠܟܺܝܢ	ܟܢܘܫܐ	ܟܢܘܫܳܢ
emphatic	ܡܰܠܟܳܐ	ܡܰܠܟܶܐ	ܟܢܘܫܬܐ	ܟܢܘܫܳܬܐ
construct	ܡܠܟ	ܡܠܟܰܝ	ܟܢܘܫܰܬ	ܟܢܘܫܳܬ

A few nouns are more or less indeclinable, notably foreign words like ܐܘܢܓܠܝܘܢ (εὐαγγέλιον) 'gospel'. The plurals of these words have to be learned individually.

The nouns and adjectives dealt with in this lesson are the simplest kind, in which the inflection does not change the vocalization of the stem. Other nouns and adjectives, with 'variable vowels', are treated in §§9-11, but some will be met in their ordinary emphatic form before that.

Nouns in the absolute state are used in three main constructions: after numbers (see §29); after the words ܟܠ 'every' and ܕܠܐ 'without'; and in some set phrases especially where the noun is repeated. Examples are:

ܟܠ ܡܕܝܢܐ	every city
ܬܪܝܢ ܟܬܒܝܢ	two books
ܟܐܦ ܥܠ ܟܐܦ	stone upon stone
ܕܠܐ ܠܫܢ	without a language.

Examples of phrases using the construct state are:

ܒܢܝ ܡܕܝܢܬܐ	the people (*lit.* sons) of the city
ܪܝܫ ܕܝܪܐ	head of the monastery – abbot.

An adjective that is attributive (as in 'the good king') goes after the noun, and agrees with it in gender, number and state. An adjective that is in the predicate (as in 'the king is good') will be in the absolute state, agreeing with its referent in number and gender. Adjectives in the predicate can take enclitic pronouns in the same way as nouns. Thus:

ܫܠܝܚܐ ܩܕܝܫܐ	the holy apostles
ܩܕܝܫܝܢ ܐܢܘܢ ܫܠܝܚܐ *or* ܩܕܝܫܝܢ ܫܠܝܚܐ	The apostles are holy.

Some feminine nouns look, and are inflected, as if they were masculine, e.g. ܟܺܐܦܳܐ 'stone', pl. ܟܺܐܦܶ̈ܐ. (This is notably the case with parts of the body that are in pairs, e.g., ܐܺܝܕܳܐ 'hand'.) Some other feminine nouns look masculine just in the plural, e.g. ܡܶܠܬ݂ܳܐ 'word', pl. ܡܶܠܶ̈ܐ. Remember, however, that any adjective modifying a feminine noun must also be feminine, e.g., ܡܶܠܶ̈ܐ ܩܰܕܺܝܫܳܬ݂ܳܐ 'holy words'.

Vocabulary[2]

ܟܺܐܢ	just (*adj.*) upright	ܐܺܝܕܳܐ	hand (*f.*)
ܣܳܒ݂	old (*of a person*)	ܪܰܒ	great; *f.* ܪܰܒ݁ܬܳܐ
ܫܰܦܺܝܪ	beautiful, fine often used in moral sense	ܪܺܫܳܐ	head, chief
ܒܺܝܫ	evil	ܡܶܠܬ݂ܳܐ	word (*f.*); *pl.* ܡܶܠܶ̈ܐ
ܫܰܪܺܝܪ	true real	ܛܳܒ݂	good
ܩܰܕܺܝܫ	holy	ܠܳܐ	not
ܚܰܟܺܝܡ	wise	ܕܠܳܐ	without
ܛܽܘܒܳܢܳܐ	blessed one (*m.*)	ܡܫܺܝܚܳܐ	Christ Messiah
ܟܺܐܦܳܐ	stone (*f.*)	ܐܶܘܰܢܓܶܠܺܝܘܢ	gospel
ܬܰܠܡܺܝܕܳܐ	disciple	ܫܠܺܝܚܳܐ	apostle (St Paul)
ܒܪܺܝܟ݂	blessed		

Exercises

Translate into English:

1. *a*. ܓܰܒ݂ܪܳܐ ܣܳܒ݂ܳܐ *b*. ܣܳܒ݂ ܓܰܒ݂ܪܳܐ.

2. ܐܶܘܰܢܓܶܠܺܝܘܢ ܩܰܕܺܝܫܳܐ ; ܡܰܠܟ݁ܽܘܬ݂ܳܐ ܫܡܰܝܳܢܬܳܐ ; ܓܰܒ݂ܪܳܐ ܚܰܟܺܝܡܳܐ.

[2] In the vocabularies from now on, adjectives appear in the masculine absolute state, and nouns in the emphatic.

3. ܡ̈ܠܐ ܕܡܫܝ̈ܚܐ ܠܬ̈ܠܡܝܕܐ ܒܥܘܠܐ ܡܛܠ ܐܢܝܢ.

4. ܡܢܘ ܐܠܟܣܢܕܪܐ ܡܠܟܐ. ܗܘܝܘ ܥܒܕܐ ܕܐܠܗܐ.

5. ܠܒܢ ܘܡܠܦܢܝܢ ܐܢܘܢ ܦܘܩܕܢܐ ܕܐܠܗܐ.

6. ܡܠܦܢܝܬܐ: ܢܫ̈ܝܢ ܡ̈ܠܐ ܗܠܝܢ.

7. ܟܢܫܝܢ ܐܝܟܢ ܕܡܠܟܘܬܐ ܐܢܘܢ ܕܫܪܪܐ.

8. ܣܦܪܐ ܦܠܐ ܩܐܦ ܕܒܡܕܝܢܬܐ.

9. ܟܢܫܐ ܡܕܝܢܬܐ ܗܕܐ. ܟܬܒܐ ܗܘ ܕܐܠܗܐ.

10. ܣܦܣܪܝܢ ܐܢܘܢ ܕܒܗ̇ ܡܕܝܢܬܐ.

Translate into Syriac:

1. a wise woman; wise women. 2. a word in the book of the holy apostle. 3. The commandments of the law are holy and just and true. 4. We are disciples of Moses and not of the Evil One. 5. The words of the gospel are true in every language. 6. The blessed ones are in the hand of God. 7. Who are the true apostles in this city? 8. This is the book of the great teacher (*m*.). 9. What is the law of Christ? It is a just law. 10. The law and the gospel are in these blessed books. 11. Which woman is in the book of holy women?

3-7

6. PRONOMINAL SUFFIXES

When the possessive case of a pronoun is used in English (e.g. '*my* book'), it is represented in Syriac by a shortened form of the pronoun attached as a suffix to the noun it qualifies. There are two sets of these suffixes, called 'singular' and 'plural' for short – these names referring to the noun taking the suffix, not the pronominal suffix itself.

The 'singular' suffixes are as follows. They are attached to all singular nouns, and also to feminine plural nouns.

	singular	plural
1st	ܝ	ܢ
2nd masc.	ܟ݂	ܟ݂ܘܢ
2nd fem.	ܟܝ	ܟܝܢ
3rd masc.	ܗ	ܗܘܢ
3rd fem.	ܗ̇	ܗܝܢ

The 'plural' suffixes, attached to masculine plural nouns, are as follows:

	singular	plural
1st	ܝ	ܝܢ
2nd masc.	ܝܟ݂	ܝܟ݂ܘܢ
2nd fem.	ܝܟܝ	ܝܟܝܢ
3rd masc.	ܘܗܝ	ܝܗܘܢ
3rd fem.	ܝܗ̇	ܝܗܝܢ

Notice the diacritical point which must be written over the ܗ of the 3rd feminine singular in both sets of suffixes.

The suffixes are attached to nouns after dropping the ܐ-
from the end of the emphatic state. The following shows
suffixes attached to the singular and plural of a masculine
noun (with invariable vowels), ܟܬܒܐ, pl. ܟܬܒܐ.

	sing. pronoun		pl. pronoun	
1st	ܟܬܒܝ	my book	ܟܬܒܢ	our book
2nd m.	ܟܬܒܟ	your "	ܟܬܒܟܘܢ	your "
2nd f.	ܟܬܒܟܝ	your "	ܟܬܒܟܝܢ	your "
3rd m.	ܟܬܒܗ	his "	ܟܬܒܗܘܢ	their "
3rd f.	ܟܬܒܗ	her "	ܟܬܒܗܝܢ	their "
1st	ܟܬܒܝ	my books	ܟܬܒܝܢ	our books
2nd m.	ܟܬܒܝܟ	your "	ܟܬܒܝܟܘܢ	your "
2nd f.	ܟܬܒܝܟܝ	your "	ܟܬܒܝܟܝܢ	your "
3rd m.	ܟܬܒܘܗܝ	his "	ܟܬܒܝܗܘܢ	their "
3rd f.	ܟܬܒܝܗ	her "	ܟܬܒܝܗܝܢ	their "

Notice the pronunciation of some of these forms:

ܟܬܒܝ	*ktab* (the suffix ܝ is not pronounced)
ܟܬܒܟ	*ktabek* and
ܟܬܒܝܟ	*ktabayk* (final ܝ not pronounced)
ܟܬܒܘܗܝ	*ktabaw* (neither ܗ nor final ܝ pronounced).

Feminine nouns also drop the ܐ- before adding suffixes.
Thus, ܟܢܘܫܬܐ 'synagogue', pl. ܟܢܘܫܬܐ :

	sing. pronoun		pl. pronoun	
1st	ܟܢܘܫܬܝ	my synagogue	ܟܢܘܫܬܢ	our synagogue
2nd m.	ܟܢܘܫܬܟ	your "	ܟܢܘܫܬܟܘܢ	your "
2nd f.	ܟܢܘܫܬܟܝ	your "	ܟܢܘܫܬܟܝܢ	your "
3rd m.	ܟܢܘܫܬܗ	his "	ܟܢܘܫܬܗܘܢ	their "
3rd f.	ܟܢܘܫܬܗ	her "	ܟܢܘܫܬܗܝܢ	their "

1st	ܟܢܘ̈ܫܳܬ̣ܝ	my synagogues	ܟܢܘ̈ܫܳܬ̣ܲܢ	our synagogues
2nd m.	ܟܢܘ̈ܫܳܬ̣ܳܟ	your "	ܟܢܘ̈ܫܳܬ̣ܟ̣ܘܢ	your "
2nd f.	ܟܢܘ̈ܫܳܬ̣ܶܟ̣ܝ	your "	ܟܢܘ̈ܫܳܬ̣ܟ̣ܝܢ	your "
3rd m.	ܟܢܘ̈ܫܳܬ̣ܗ	his "	ܟܢܘ̈ܫܳܬ̣ܗܘܢ	their "
3rd f.	ܟܢܘ̈ܫܳܬ̣ܳܗ	her "	ܟܢܘ̈ܫܳܬ̣ܗܝܢ	their "

The same remarks about pronunciation apply to the feminine forms: ܟܢܘܫܟܝ is *knušt*, etc.

The genitive relation may be expressed in Syriac in three ways: using the construct state; using the emphatic state together with the relative -ܕ; and by the use of both the possessive pronominal suffix and -ܕ. Thus 'the teacher's book' may be ܟܬܳܒ̣ ܡܲܠܦ̣ܳܢܳܐ or ܟܬܳܒ̣ܳܐ ܕܡܲܠܦ̣ܳܢܳܐ or ܟܬܳܒ̣ܶܗ ܕܡܲܠܦ̣ܳܢܳܐ. The last of these is very common.

Vocabulary

ܫܡܲܝܳܐ	heaven (pl)	ܡܲܠܦ̣ܳܢܽܘܬ̣ܳܐ	doctrine *teaching*
ܟܢܘ̈ܫܬܳܐ	synagogue	ܢܒ̣ܝܳܐ	prophet
ܫܠܳܡܳܐ	peace	ܠܳܐ	not (= ܗ̱ܘ ܠܳܐ)
ܦܘܡܳܐ	mouth	ܐܲܪܥܳܐ	land, earth (*f.*);
ܥܘܡܪܳܐ	monastery (*f.*) *sheepfold orig.*	*pl.* ܐܲܪ̈ܥܳܬ̣ܳܐ	
pl. ܥܘܡܪ̈ܶܐ		ܠܶܒܳܐ	heart *thinking organ*
ܣܲܓܝ̈ܐܝܢ	many (*pl.*);	ܕܘܒܳܪ̈ܶܐ	way of life (*pl.*)
emph. ܣܲܓܝ̈ܐܢܶܐ		ܝܗܘܕܳܝܳܐ	Jew
ܥܺܕܬܳܐ	church (*f.*)	ܝܲܘܢܳܝ	Greek (*adj.*) *sand ancient Gk*
pl. ܥܺܕܳ̈ܬܳܐ		ܟܪܺܣܛܝܳܢܳܐ	Christian (*adj.*)

customary practices that go
to make up your
way of life.

Exercises

Translate into English:

Translate into Syriac, using suffixed forms where possible:

1. the law of God (*write this in three ways*).   2. the land of the Jews.   3. the doctrines of the Greeks.   4. Is his teacher not a prophet?   5. His way of life is good and true. 6. Words of peace are in her mouth and in her heart. 7. You (*m.*) are evil prophets and your words are not true. 8. Heaven and earth are God's.   9. The synagogues of that land are many.   10. The church of the Christians in the city is fine.

7. PREPOSITIONS. THE WORDS -ܕܝܼܠ AND ܐܝܼܬ

In §4 we dealt with the prepositions -ܒ -ܕ -ܠ, which are prefixed to their objects. Other prepositions are separate words, as in English.

When a preposition has a pronoun as its object, the appropriate pronominal suffix is attached to the preposition in the same way as to a noun. Some prepositions take the 'singular' suffixes, others the 'plural'. The following are some of the most important prepositions. (Prepositions with 'variable vowels' will appear in §11.)

-ܒ 'in, with'. Singular suffixes are attached, to give ܒܝܼ, ܒܳܟ, ܒܶܟܝ, ܒܶܗ, ܒܳܗ̇, ܒܰܢ, ܒܟܽܘܢ, ܒܟܶܝܢ, ܒܗܽܘܢ, ܒܗܶܝܢ. Note the vowel on ܒܝܼ which makes it pronounceable.

-ܠ 'to, for'. Singular suffixes: ܠܝܼ etc. (as for -ܒ). -ܠ is also used before the definite direct object of a verb (see §8).

ܡܶܢ 'from'. Singular suffixes: ܡܶܢܝ, ܡܶܢܳܟ, ܡܶܢܶܟܝ, ܡܶܢܶܗ, etc. Also expressed with ܡܶܢ are the comparative and partitive:

ܛܳܒ ܡܶܢ ܕܰܗܒܳܐ ܣܰܓܺܝܐܳ	better than fine gold
ܐܰܝܢܳܐ ܡܶܢܟܽܘܢ	which of you?

ܥܰܡ 'along with'. Singular suffixes: ܥܰܡܝ ('am) 'with me', etc.

ܡܶܛܽܠ 'because of, for the sake of'. Singular suffixes are attached to the form -ܡܶܛܽܠܳܬ; thus,

ܡܶܛܽܠܳܬܰܢ ܘܡܶܛܽܠ ܦܽܘܪܩܳܢܰܢ for us and for our salvation.

With -ܕ added, ܡܛܠ becomes the conjunction 'because':

ܡܛܠ ܕܫܠܝܚܐ ܐܢܐ   because I am an apostle.

ܒܝܬ, ܒܝܢܝ 'among, between'. ܒܝܢܝ takes singular suffixes;
for ܒܝܬ plural suffixes are attached to the form -ܒܝܢܝ.
Thus: ܒܝܢܬܗܘܢ or ܒܝܢܬܗܘܢ 'among them'. Notice also

ܒܝܢܝ ܘܠܟ   between me and you.

Another form of this preposition is ܒܝܬ (unrelated to
'house'), not used with suffixes.

ܠܘܬ 'at, with, near, in the presence of, among; to, toward'.
Singular suffixes: e.g., ܫܠܡܐ ܠܘܬܢ ܘܠܘܬ ܐܠܗܐ 'peace
among ourselves and toward God'.

ܐܝܟ 'like, as'; pronounced ak. Singular suffixes are attached
to the form -ܐܟܘܬ; thus ܐܟܘܬܝ, ܐܟܘܬܟ, ܐܟܘܬܗ, etc.

ܥܠ 'upon, over, concerning, unto'. Plural suffixes are
attached to the form -ܥܠ (with no vowel); thus ܥܠܢ,
ܥܠܟܘܢ, ܥܠܝܗܘܢ, etc.

ܬܚܝܬ 'under'. Plural suffixes are most usually attached to a
different form, -ܬܚܘܬ; e.g.

ܥܠ ܐܪܥܐ ܘܬܚܘܬܝܗ   on the earth and under it.

ܩܕܡ 'before', either in space or in time. Plural suffixes.

-ܕܝܠ. The preposition -ܕ does not take suffixes, but singular
suffixes are attached to the form -ܕܝܠ to make an emphatic possessive. For example,

ܟܬܒܐ ܕܝܠܝ or ܟܬܒܐ ܕܝܠܝ   my own book
ܕܝܠܗ ܗܘ ܐܪܥܐ.   the land is his.

ܐ݂ܝܬ may be included in this list, although it is more like a verb than a preposition. Without a suffix, it means 'there is' or 'there are'. The negative is ܠܝܬ (= ܐ݂ܝܬ ܠܐ) 'there is not'. Used with the preposition ܠـ it takes on the meaning 'to have'. Examples are:

ܠܝܬ ܡܰܝܳܐ ܐܰܡܢ   there is no water there

ܐ݂ܝܬ ܠܢ ܢܳܡܘܣܐ   we have a law.

With suffixes (always plural), however, ܐ݂ܝܬ functions as a linking verb. This construction is an alternative to the simple personal pronoun learned in §4. Thus:

ܡܰܠܟܐ ܐ݂ܝܬܰܝܟ   you are king

ܟܪ̈ܣܛܝܢܐ ܐ݂ܝܬܰܝܗܘܢ   they are Christians.

ܟܠ when used with suffixes (singular) means 'all' or 'the whole', and any following noun must be in the emphatic state. Notice the different expressions

ܟܠ ܟܬܒ   every book

ܟܠܗ ܟܬܒܐ   the whole book

ܟܠܗܘܢ ܟܬܒ̈ܐ   all the books.

Vocabulary

ܪܘܚܐ	spirit, wind (f.); pl. usu. ܪ̈ܘܚܐ	ܦܘܪܩܢܐ	salvation
ܗܝܡܢܘܬܐ	faith (f.)	ܡܕܡ	something, what
ܡܰܝܳܐ	water (pl.)	ܟܠ ܡܕܡ	everything
ܗܝܟܠܐ	temple, palace	ܐܰܡܢ	there
ܡܪܐ	lord; cstr. ܡܪܐ	ܛܝܒܘܬܐ	grace, favour (f.)
ܡܪܝܐ	the Lord	ܕܝܢܐ	judge
		ܡܛܠ ܡܢܐ	why?

Exercises

Translate into English:

1. ܒܟܝ ; ܡܛܠܗܕܐ ; ܐܟܘܬܟ ; ܩܕܡܝܗܘܢ
2. ܟܠ ܡܕܡ ܕܐܝܬ ܠܫܡܐ ܫܡܝܐ
3. ܒܢܝܐ ܐܝܬ ܠܗ ܠܡܠܟܐ ܕܐܝܬ ܒܗ ܕܗܒܐ ܒܣܝܡܐ.
4. ܡܪܢܐ ܐܠܗܢ ܗܘ ܐܝܬܘܗܝ ܡܪܐ ܟܠ.
5. ܠܝܬ ܥܒܕܐ ܕܪܒ ܡܢ ܡܪܗ: ܘܠܐ ܬܠܡܝܕܐ ܕܡܝܬܪ ܡܢ ܡܠܦܢܗ.
6. ܐܝܬ ܕܘܟܬܐ ܡܫܝܢܬܐ: ܘܡܠܟܐ ܗܘ ܕܐܝܬܘܗܝ ܕܝܠܐ ܒܝܠܕܘܗܝ.
7. ܠܝܬܘܗܝ ܢܒܝܐ ܒܪܢܫܐ ܡܛܠ ܕܫܪܪܐ ܠܝܬ ܒܗ.
8. ܒܫܡܝܐ ܕܐܠܗܐ ܐܝܬ ܡܕܡ ܕܐܝܬ.
9. ܡܪܝ ܐܢܬ ܡܛܠ ܕܐܝܬ ܠܟ ܫܘܠܛܢܐ.
10. ܐܝܬ ܒܓܘܐ ܕܝܠܟ ܐܦ ܕܐܝܬ ܕܝܠܝ.

Translate into Syriac. Use ܐܝܬ + suffix where possible.

1. Unto him; from you (*f. sing.*); before her; for my sake. 2. Everything that is in the water and under it. 3. There is a city in which there is a beautiful palace. 4. You blessed ones have the spirit of God among you. 5. I am queen of this city. 6. The land is not ours, and we have no peace. 7. Every city has a synagogue. All kings have wives. 8. We have a wise God. Is there a God like him? 9. Lord, you are the judge of all of us. 10. All my doctrine I have from my teacher.

8. VERBS. THE PERFECT TENSE

As in other Semitic languages, verbs in Syriac have a root,
or stem, consisting of three letters, or 'radicals'. (Some exceptions will appear in §16.) The inflection of the verb is by
means of different vowels or doubling applied to these radicals, and by suffixes ('afformatives') and prefixes ('preformatives'). These inflections indicate: 1. conjugation; 2.
tense; and 3. number, person, and gender.

1. Conjugations, a feature of Semitic languages, correspond
somewhat to the inflections known as 'voices' in Indo-
European languages, but they have a wider scope. The
names of the conjugations are based on the verb ܦܠܚ ('to
labour') and each name comes from the way that conjugation modifies the three root letters. The names and meanings of the six principal conjugations in Syriac are thus as
follows:

pe'al	the simple form of the verb;
ethpe'el	the passive of the simple form;
pa'el	the intensive;
ethpa'al	the passive of the intensive;
aph'el	the causative;
ettaph'al	the passive of the causative.[1]

(Some other less common conjugations will be met in §17.)

---

[1] These names are spelled conventionally. More correctly they
would be: *p'al, etp'el, pa''el, etpa''al, ap'el, ettap'al.*

The verb used in paradigms is not ܩܛܠ but ܩܛܠ 'to kill'. This verb does not actually appear in all the six conjugations (nor, probably, does any other verb), but it is useful to keep the same root throughout the next few lessons. The various conjugations of ܩܛܠ look like this in their basic form, the 3rd masc. sing. perfect:

	active	passive
simple	ܩܛܰܠ	?ܐܬܩܛܶܠ
intensive	ܩܰܛܶܠ	?ܐܬܩܰܛܰܠ
causative	?ܐܩܛܶܠ	?ܐܬܐܩܛܰܠ

The verb ܩܛܠ is a 'strong' verb: all the root letters are ordinary consonants (not *alaph, waw, yod*) and the third is not a double of the second. Many other verbs are 'weak'. These fall into classes known as, for example, *pe-yod* verbs, in which the first radical (corresponding to *pe* in ܩܛܠ) is the weak letter *yod*. In this book the strong verb is treated in all its conjugations first, then each class of weak verb in turn.

2. Within each conjugation there are properly two tenses, called perfect and imperfect. The perfect corresponds roughly to the past, and the imperfect to the future. The present is usually expressed by the participle, which is not, formally, considered a 'tense' (see §10). The other forms of the verb are the infinitive and the imperative.

3. The perfect and imperfect (the so-called 'finite' forms of the verb) are inflected to make the same distinctions of gender, number, and person as the personal pronouns.

The perfect. This is inflected by adding to the stem the following afformatives:

	sing.	pl.
3rd masc.	—	ه
3rd fem.	ܰܬ ′	—
2nd masc.	ܬ	ܐܬܘ
2nd fem.	ܬܝ	ܝܢ
1st	ܬ ்	ܢ

The pe'al perfect of ܩܛܠ is then as follows:

	sing.			pl.	
ܩܛܰܠ	he killed		ܩܛܰܠܘ	they (*m.*) killed
ܩܶܛܠܰܬ	she killed		ܩܛܰܠ	they (*f.*) killed
ܩܛܰܠܬ	you (*m.*) killed		ܩܛܰܠܬܘܢ	you (*m.*) killed
ܩܛܰܠܬܝ	you (*f.*) killed		ܩܛܰܠܬܝܢ	you (*f.*) killed
ܩܶܛܠܶܬ	I killed		ܩܛܰܠܢ	we killed.

The ending ه- on the 3rd m. pl. is not pronounced. The 2nd m. and f. sing. are both pronounced *qtalt*. The 1st pl. is *qtaln*. It will be seen that in the 3rd f. sing. and the 1st sing. the vowel is shifted to the first radical. If the third radical is a *bgdkpt* letter, it then takes *qushaya*; e.g. ܟܶܬܒܶܬ 'I wrote'.

The 3rd fem. pl. of the perfect is curiously identical to the 3rd masc. sing. This is the form in older manuscripts and in the East Syriac tradition. In later West Syriac texts it is ܩܛܰܠܝ̈, a spelling intended to distinguish it in writing from ܩܛܰܠ, but still pronounced *qtal*.

There are longer forms of the 1st and 3rd plural that distinguish them in pronunciation. These forms, which are not very common, are:

ܩܛܰܠܢܰܢ for ܩܛܰܠܢ
ܩܛܰܠܘܢ for ܩܛܰܠܘ
ܩܛܰܠܝ̈ܢ for ܩܛܰܠ or ܩܛܰܠܝ̈.

A number of verbs, like ܕܚܶܠ 'to fear, be afraid', have the vowel *e* instead of *a* in the perfect, and so appear as follows:

	sing.	pl.
3rd m. sing.	ܕܚܶܠ	ܕܚܶܠܘ or ܕܚܶܠܘܢ
3rd f. sing.	ܕܶܚܠܰܬ	ܕܚܶܠ (ܕܚܶܠܝ̈) or ܕܚܶܠܝ̈ܢ
2nd m. sing.	ܕܚܶܠܬ	ܕܚܶܠܬܘܢ
2nd f. sing.	ܕܚܶܠܬܝ	ܕܚܶܠܬܶܝܢ
1st	ܕܶܚܠܶܬ	ܕܚܶܠܢ or ܕܚܶܠܢܰܢ

Verbs in *a* like ܩܛܰܠ are mostly transitive. Those in *e* like ܕܚܶܠ are mostly intransitive. There are exceptions, like ܢܦܰܠ 'to fall' and ܣܓܶܕ 'to worship'. Verbs with a guttural letter (ܗ, ܚ, or ܥ) or ܪ for the third radical always have the vowel *a* rather than *e*, even if intransitive like ܬܡܰܗ 'to wonder'.

Syntax. There are no hard and fast rules about the order of words in a Syriac sentence. Very generally, if the subject is short, then the predicate, or at least the verb, goes first; but the subject or some other part of the sentence may be moved forward for emphasis.

ܕܚܶܠ ܡܰܠܟܳܐ ܡܶܢ ܟܶܢܫܳܐ.	The king feared the crowd.
ܐܶܓܰܪܬܳܐ ܟܬܰܒ ܘܠܳܐ ܟܬܳܒܳܐ.	He wrote a letter, not a book.

The particle ܠ- often introduces a direct object that is definite (in English, *the* instead of *a*). Thus:

ܢܣܰܒܢ ܦܽܘܩܕܳܢܳܐ ܡܶܢ ܐܰܠܳܗܳܐ.	We received a commandment from God.

ܢܛܪܢ ܠܦܘܩܕܢܐ ܕܢܣܒܢ. We have kept the commandment that we received.

If the object is a pronoun, ܠ- takes the appropriate suffix. The personal pronouns cannot be used as objects of verbs, except ܐܢܘܢ and ܐܢܝܢ. Thus 'he kept them' may be expressed by either ܢܛܪ ܐܢܘܢ or ܢܛܪ ܠܗܘܢ.

Vocabulary[2]

ܟܬܒ	write	ܟܢܫܐ	crowd
ܩܛܠ	kill	ܦܐܪܐ	fruit
ܕܚܠ (ܡܢ)	fear, be afraid (of)	ܡܬܠܐ	parable
ܫܡܥ	hear	ܝܫܘܥ	Jesus
ܥܒܕ	do, make	ܐܓܪܬܐ	letter
ܢܛܪ	keep	ܟܕ	when, while
ܬܡܗ	wonder	ܐܘܪܫܠܡ	Jerusalem
ܢܣܒ	take, receive	ܡܪܝܡ	Mary
ܥܒܪ	cross, transgress	ܩܠܐ	voice
ܣܓܕ	worship	ܛܠܝܘܬܐ	childhood (*f.*)
ܢܦܠ	fall	ܐܕܡ	Adam
ܚܘܐ	Eve		

Exercises

Translate into English:

1. ܐܕܡ ܘܚܘܐ ܥܒܪܘ ܥܠܘܗܝ ܥܠ ܦܘܩܕܢܗ ܕܐܠܗܐ.
2. ܟܠܗܘܢ ܗܠܝܢ ܦܘܩܕܢܐ ܢܛܪܬ ܡܢ ܛܠܝܘܬܝ.

[2] In the vocabularies, weak verbs may appear whose full conjugation has to await later lessons (here ܢܛܪ, ܢܣܒ, ܢܦܠ; see §20). The exercises use only forms of these verbs that are regular.

3. ܫܡܥܢ ܡܢ ܢܡܘܣܐ ܕܡܫܝܚܐ ܐܒܘܗܝ ܕܡܠܟܐ ܗܘ.

4. ܫܡܥܬܘܢ ܠܡܠܬܐ ܕܥܠ ܕܝܢܐ ܥܡܐ ܘܐܝܟܢܐ ܫܒܩܬܐ.

5. ܦܩܕܬ ܠܟܘܢ ܡܛܠ ܗܝܡܢܘܬܐ ܕܐܠܗ ܠܥܡܟܘܢ.

6. ܫܡܥܬ ܥܠ ܗܝܡܢܘܬܟܘܢ ܘܥܠ ܗܘ ܕܚܙܝܬ ܒܥܒܕܝܟܘܢ ܠܗܘ
ܩܕܡܝܐ.

7. ܡܪܝܡ ܢܛܪܬ ܟܠܗܝܢ ܡ̈ܠܐ ܗܠܝܢ ܒܠܒܗ.

8. ܡܬܠܗ ܠܡܠܟܐ ܕܠܥܒܕܘܗܝ ܐܚܪܢܘܗܝ ܘܫܒܩܗ ܡܕܝܢܬܐ.

9. ܐܘܪܫܠܡ ܐܘܪܫܠܡ ܩܛܠܬ ܠܢܒܝܐ.

10. ܐܡܪܘܗܝ ܥܠ ܦܠܚܝܢ ܕܥܒܕܘ ܫܟܝܢܬܐ ܘܥܠ ܡܠܟܘܬܗܘܢ.

Translate into Syriac:

1. We have a letter that fell from heaven. 2. Adam and Eve were afraid when they heard the voice of God near them. 3. The women wrote many fine words to the king. 4. God did not keep Jerusalem from the Greeks. 5. In my youth I did not fear God. 6. When I heard those words I fell (down) and worshipped. 7. This fruit that I have is from her, the woman that you made. 8. In Jesus's parable, who are the servants and who is the master? 9. We have heard the commandments of the apostles and have done them. 10. What did he write concerning those who transgressed against the law of Moses?

9. SIMPLE NOUNS WITH VARIABLE VOWELS

Unlike the nouns seen in §5 (such as ܟܬܒܐ and ܡܠܟܘܬܐ), many nouns change the pattern of their vowels when inflected. This lesson deals with the nouns in this class that have three root letters but only one short vowel besides the ܵ- or ܵܐ- of the emphatic state. The masculine and feminine nouns of this kind behave differently.

Masculine-type nouns. Examples are ܟܠܒܐ (with the vowel *a*), ܦܓܪܐ 'body' (with *u*), and ܪܓܠܐ 'foot' (with *e*). (Like some other nouns of this kind, ܪܓܠܐ is actually feminine.)

In the inflection of these nouns, the only difference from nouns like ܟܬܒܐ is in the absolute and construct singular. In these two forms, which are the same, the vowel is on the second root letter instead of the first. Usually this vowel is *e*; thus, ܟܠܒ, ܪܓܠ. But there are exceptions.

a. When the third root letter is a guttural or ܪ, the vowel is *a*, as in ܒܣܪ (abs. of ܒܣܪܐ 'flesh').

b. When the vowel in the emphatic state is *u*, this vowel is kept, as in ܦܓܘܪ (abs. of ܦܓܪܐ).

c. Some words that had historically two vowels (e.g. ܕܗܒܐ 'gold', from an original *dahabā*) keep the vowel *a*; thus, ܕܗܒ. Another example is ܙܒܢ (abs. of ܙܒܢܐ 'time').

Notice also that, following the rule on p. 14, words starting with ܒ or ܐ need to be supplied with an initial vowel in the absolute and construct. So we have for example ܐܽܘܪܰܚ (abs. of ܐܽܘܪܚܳܐ) and ܝܰܪܰܚ (abs. of ܝܰܪܚܳܐ 'month').

Pronominal suffixes are added to these nouns in the familiar way and there is no change of vowels. On ܡܰܠܟܳܐ, for example, the suffixes are ܡܰܠܟܝ, ܡܰܠܟܳܟ, ܡܰܠܟܶܟܝ, ܡܰܠܟܶܗ, ܡܰܠܟܳܗ, ܡܰܠܟܰܢ, ܡܰܠܟܟܽܘܢ, ܡܰܠܟܟܶܝܢ, ܡܰܠܟܗܽܘܢ, ܡܰܠܟܗܶܝܢ. Notice the forms that have clusters of consonants: the 1st singular is pronounced *malk*, and the 2nd and 3rd plural are *malkkon*, *malkken*, etc. The plural suffixes are also straightforward: ܡܰܠܟܰܝ, ܡܰܠܟܰܝܟ, ܡܰܠܟܰܝܟܝ etc.

Feminine nouns. These have the vowel on the second root letter only in the emphatic singular. In all the other forms it moves to the first root letter. Thus the following paradigm is produced. The examples are ܚܰܒܪܬܳܐ 'companion' (with the vowel *a*; the fem. of ܚܰܒܪܳܐ 'male companion'), ܥܶܓܠܬܳܐ 'heifer' (with the vowel *e*), and ܡܫܽܘܚܬܳܐ 'measure' (with *u*).

sing.			pl.		
emph.	abs.	cstr.	emph.	abs.	cstr.
ܚܰܒܪܬܳܐ	ܚܰܒܪܳܐ	ܚܰܒܪܰܬ	ܚܰܒܪܳܬܳܐ	ܚܰܒܪܳܢ	ܚܰܒܪܳܬ
ܥܶܓܠܬܳܐ	ܥܶܓܠܳܐ	ܥܶܓܠܰܬ	ܥܶܓܠܳܬܳܐ	ܥܶܓܠܳܢ	ܥܶܓܠܳܬ
ܡܫܽܘܚܬܳܐ	ܡܫܽܘܚܳܐ	ܡܫܽܘܚܰܬ	ܡܫܽܘܚܳܬܳܐ	ܡܫܽܘܚܳܢ	ܡܫܽܘܚܳܬ

The vowel that appears in the other states is usually the same one (*a*, *e*, or *u*) as in the emphatic singular; but there are exceptions, like ܬܶܢܚܳܐ, abs. of ܬܰܢܚܬܳܐ 'groan', so one other form of these words needs to be learned along with the emphatic singular.

Suffixes are added to this group of nouns in the usual way, by removing the ending from the emphatic state. There is no further change of vowels. Thus for example: ܣܟ݂ܒܝ 'my companion', ܣܟ݂ܒܐܟ݂ 'your (*m. sing.*) companion', ܣܚܒܝ 'my companions', ܣܚܒܝܟܝܢ 'your (*f. pl.*) companions', etc.

It is convenient to deal here with another set of feminine nouns which look similar, although strictly speaking they have 'invariable' vowels. Examples are ܡܠܟܬܐ, ܘܣܠܬܐ 'fear', and ܚܕܘܬܐ 'blessing'. In these words, the vowel stays on the first root letter throughout the inflection. Thus:

	sing.			pl.	
emph.	abs.	cstr.	emph.	abs.	cstr.
ܡܠܟܬܐ	ܡܠܟܐ	ܡܠܟܬ	ܡܠܟܬܐ	ܡܠܟܢ	ܡܠܟܬ
ܘܣܠܬܐ	ܘܣܠܐ	ܘܣܠܬ	ܘܣܠܬܐ	ܘܣܠܢ	ܘܣܠܬ
ܚܕܘܬܐ	ܚܕܘܐ	ܚܕܘܬ	ܚܕܘܬܐ	ܚܕܘܢ	ܚܕܘܬ

These forms are all regular. With suffixes, however, there is a variation: on singular nouns an extra vowel *a* appears before the 1st sing. and the 2nd and 3rd pl. suffixes. The suffixed forms of ܡܠܟܬܐ are thus:

ܡܠܟܬܝ	my queen	ܡܠܟܬܢ	our queen
ܡܠܟܬܟ݂	your (*m.*) queen	ܡܠܟܬܟ݂ܘܢ	your (*m. pl.*) queen
ܡܠܟܬܟ݂ܝ	your (*f.*) queen	ܡܠܟܬܟ݂ܝܢ	your (*f. pl.*) queen
ܡܠܟܬܗ	his queen	ܡܠܟܬܗܘܢ	their (*m. pl.*) queen
ܡܠܟܬܗ	her queen	ܡܠܟܬܗܝܢ	their (*f. pl.*) queen.

Various other feminine nouns that are otherwise inflected regularly like ܣܢܐܬܐ also follow this pattern of suffixes. These are words in which the suffixes produce a cluster of consonants that is then resolved by the extra vowel: e.g.,

ܡܕܝܢܬܝ (not ܡܕܝܢܝܬܝ) 'my city', ܐܢܬܬܝ (not ܐܢܬܬܝ) 'my wife',
and ܡܠܬܝ (*mellaṯ*; the *lamad* is doubled[1]) 'my word'.

With all these feminine nouns, the suffixes on the plural are
regular: ܡܠܟܬܝ 'my queens', ܡܠܟܬܟܘܢ 'your queens', etc.

Vocabulary

ܚܫܒ	(think), suppose	ܥܪܩ	flee
ܩܪܒ	draw near	ܒܥܠܕܒܒܐ	enemy
ܚܒܪܐ	companion;	ܗܪܟܐ	here
	fem. ܚܒܪܬܐ	ܩܕܝܫܘܬܐ	holiness
ܕܚܠܬܐ	fear (*f.*)	ܡܫܘܚܬܐ	measure, age (*f.*)
ܒܘܪܟܬܐ	blessing (*f.*)	ܥܠܡܐ	world, age
ܕܗܒܐ	gold	ܬܘܒ	again, next
ܥܣܩ	difficult;	ܠܐ ܬܘܒ	no longer, *never again*
	emph. ܥܣܩܐ	ܢܨܒܬܐ	plant (*f.*)
ܓܘܫܡܐ	body	ܚܟܡܬܐ	wisdom (*f.*)
ܬܢܚܬܐ	groan (*f.*);	ܕܝܢ	however, <u>but</u> (*usu.*
	pl. ܬܢܚܬܐ		*2nd word in a clause*) *adversative, post-positive*

Exercises

Translate into English:

1. ܡܠܟܬܗܘܢ ; ܡܠܟܬܗ ; ܡܠܟܬܗ ; ܡܠܟܬܗ

2. ܦܠܚܘ ܗܠܝܢ ܢܨܒܬܐ ܚܦܬܝ ܐܕܡܬܗܝܢ .

3. ܕܚܠܬܐ ܘܚܒܐ ܢܗܘܐ ܥܠܐ ܩܝܡܐ ܩܘܕܗ .

---

[1] On doubled letters see Appendix A, p. 139.

Translate into Syriac:

1. Peace (be) upon you, my companions (*f.*).   2. They fled from the evils (*f.*) of the world to a monastery.   3. We Christians are in this world as the body (*use the construct*) of Christ.   4. The queen took her companion's letter and kept it.   5. I have heard about (*use* ܥܲܠ) the measure of your (*f. pl.*) faith and your wisdom.   6. Every land has a palace for its kings and queens.   7. They kept the body of the blessed one in the monastery.   8. It is a difficult parable, but (*use* ܐܸܠܵܐ) I supposed that it (was) Jesus's own words.   9. Did you (*m. sing.*) suppose that the teacher (*f.*) has many disciples? 10. You (*f. sing.*) have preserved us from our enemies.

10. PARTICIPLES

The verb in the peꜤal has an active and a passive participle.
For ܩܛܠ they are:

active	ܩܳܛܶܠ	killing, a killer
passive	ܩܛܺܝܠ	being killed, one that is killed.

Participles share some characteristics with nouns (or better,
adjectives) and some with verbs. In their inflection they are
treated like adjectives; but they often function as verbs, and
in particular they are used to express the present and other
continuous tenses.

Inflection. The forms shown above are the m. sing. absolute.
The whole inflection of the active participle is as follows:

	sing.				pl.		
	abs.	emph.	cstr.		abs.	emph.	cstr.
m.	ܩܳܛܶܠ	ܩܳܛܠܳܐ	ܩܳܛܶܠ		ܩܳܛܠܺܝܢ	ܩܳܛܠܶܐ	ܩܳܛܠܰܝ
f.	ܩܳܛܠܳܐ	ܩܳܛܶܠܬܳܐ	ܩܳܛܠܰܬ		ܩܳܛܠܳܢ	ܩܳܛܠܳܬܳܐ	ܩܳܛܠܳܬ

In these forms, the first syllable -ܩܳ is unchanging. The vowel
e on the second root letter appears just in the masculine sing.
absolute and construct, and in the feminine sing. emphatic.
When the third root letter of a verb is a guttural or ܪ, the
occasional vowel in this inflection is not *e* but *a*, as in ܢܳܛܰܪ
(not ܢܳܛܶܪ) ‘keeping’.

The *seyame* points shown on the masculine absolute plural
ܩܳܛܠܺܝܢ are written only when this form is used as a noun, and
not when it is used as a verb or adjective.

For the passive participle, the inflection is as follows:

	sing. abs.	sing. emph.	sing. cstr.	pl. abs.	pl. emph.	pl. cstr.
m.	ܩܛܝܠ	ܩܛܝܠܐ	ܩܛܝܠ	ܩܛܝܠܝܢ	ܩܛܝ̈ܠܐ	ܩܛܝ̈ܠܝ
f.	ܩܛܝܠܐ	ܩܛܝܠܬܐ	ܩܛܝܠܬ	ܩܛܝ̈ܠܢ	ܩܛܝ̈ܠܬܐ	ܩܛܝ̈ܠܬ

This inflection is just like that for ܪܫܐ or ܡܠܟܐ, that is, with no changes of vowel.

Active participles as nouns and adjectives. The active participle is formally a kind of *nomen agentis* ('agent-noun'; in English: kill*er*). It is not, however, the usual one, which in the peʿal is ܩܛܘܠܐ. (So we have, for example, ܢܛܘܪܐ 'keeper'.) The participle is more often found in such phrases as:

ܟܠ ܩܛܠ	every killer
ܥܒ̈ܕܝ ܒ̈ܝܫܬܐ	evildoers
ܡܠܟܢ ܪܚܡ ܐܠܗܐ	our God-loving emperor.

Ordinary nouns that are active participles in form usually have special meanings, e.g. ܦܪܚܬܐ 'bird' (f. ptc. of ܦܪܚ 'fly') and ܪܚܡܐ 'friend' (m. ptc. of ܪܚܡ 'love').

Active participles as verbs. In the absolute state, the active participle serves to express continuous action in the present. In the 1st and 2nd persons, the subject of the verb is denoted by the enclitic personal pronoun. Some contractions take place between the participle and the pronoun, which may also be written as one word. Thus:

ܩܛܠ ܐܢܬ	or	ܩܛܠܬ	you (*m.*) are killing
ܩܛܠܐ ܐܢܬܝ	or	ܩܛܠܬܝ	you (*f.*) are killing
ܩܛܠ ܐܢܐ	or	ܩܛܠܢܐ	I (*m.*) am killing

ܩܳܛܠܳܐ ܐ̱ܢܳܐ	or	ܩܳܛܠܳܢܳܐ	I (*f.*) am killing
ܩܳܛܠܺܝܢ ܐ̱ܢܬܽܘܢ	or	ܩܳܛܠܺܝܬܽܘܢ	you (*m. pl.*) are killing
ܩܳܛܠܳܢ ܐ̱ܢܬܶܝܢ	or	ܩܳܛܠܳܬܶܝܢ	you (*f. pl.*) are killing
ܩܳܛܠܺܝܢ ܚ̱ܢܰܢ	or	ܩܳܛܠܺܝܢܰܢ	we (*m.*) are killing
ܩܳܛܠܳܢ ܚ̱ܢܰܢ	or	ܩܳܛܠܳܢܰܢ	we (*f.*) are killing.

In the plural forms the *-n* ending of the participle is not pronounced, even if it is written. The 2nd person pl. forms are thus *qāṭliton* and *qāṭlāten* whether written as two words or one. In the 3rd person, the pronoun is omitted if the subject is simply 'he', 'she' or 'they'. Examples of active participles used in various ways as verbs are:

ܫܳܡܥܺܝܢܰܢ ܠܩܳܠܟܽܘܢ	we hear your voice
ܐܰܠܳܗܳܐ ܕܰܡܫܰܡܫܺܝܢ ܐ̱ܢܬܽܘܢ ܠܶܗ	the God whom you worship
ܕܳܚܠܳܢܳܐ ܡܶܢܳܗ̇	I (*f.*) am afraid of her
ܣܳܦܩܳܐ ܗ̱ܝ ܠܳܟ ܛܰܝܒܽܘܬܝ	my grace is sufficient for thee.

The subordination of a participle to a main verb by means of ܟܰܕ ('when, while') is very frequent, as in:

ܩܪܶܒܘ ܟܰܕ ܪܳܗܛܺܝܢ	They approached, running.

Passive participles are used in much the same way as the active. Examples are:

ܟܬܺܝܒ ܒܢܳܡܽܘܣܳܐ	it is written in the law
ܫܡܺܝܥܳܐ	one who is heard of – a famous person.

In a passive construction with the participle, the doer of the action may be introduced by ܠ-, as in

ܫܡܺܝܥ ܠܰܢ	it is heard by us – we hear
ܡܺܐܡܪܳܐ ܕܰܥܒܺܝܕ ܠܩܰܕܺܝܫܳܐ ܡܳܪܝ ܐܰܦܪܶܝܡ	a *memra* composed by the holy Mar Ephrem.

Vocabulary

ܪܗܛ	run	ܐܟܠ	eat[1]
ܐܡܪ	say[1]	ܐܟܠ ܩܪܨܐ	accuse, slander[1]
ܝܕܥ	know[1]	ܪܚܡ	love
ܣܦܩ	be enough	ܪܚܡܐ	friend (*m.*);
ܪܚܡ	love		ܪܚܡܬܐ (*f.*)
ܡܐܡܪܐ	*memra*,[2] treatise	ܢܦܫܐ	soul, self (*f.*);
ܡܪܝ	(my) lord, sir		*pl.* ܢܦܫܬܐ
	(*vocative*), Mar[3]	ܥܐܕܐ	festival
ܫܦܝܪ	well, finely	ܒܣܪܐ	flesh, meat
ܣܒܪܐ	hope	ܗܫܐ	now
ܐܦܪܝܡ	Ephrem	ܐܘ	o (*vocative*)
ܝܥܩܘܒ	Jacob, James	ܚܕ	one, a (*m.*); ܚܕܐ (*f.*)
ܦܪܚܬܐ	bird(s) (*f.*)		

Exercises

Translate into English:

1. ܠܝܬ ܠܗ ܠܥܠܡܐ ܪܚܡܐ ܒܐܘܪܚܗ ܕܚܠܗ.
2. ܟܠ ܡܢ ܕܫܡܥ ܡܠܝ ܗܠܝܢ ܘܠܐ ܥܒܕ ܠܗܘܢ ܐܝܟ ܓܒܪܐ ܗܘ ܕܐܟܠ ܒܣܪܗ.
3. ܗܫܐ ܝܕܥ ܐܢܐ ܕܪܚܡܐ ܐܢܬ ܕܐܠܗܐ.

[1] Until §§21-2 these weak verbs will be used only in their active participle forms, which are the same as for strong verbs.

[2] Or 'metrical homily', a long poetical composition in lines of equal length. The spelling *memra* is East Syriac: see p. 145.

[3] The title of a bishop or male saint. The feminine is ܡܪܬܝ.

Translate into Syriac. Use some masculine and some feminine forms.

1. My friends, what are you doing? 2. We are doers of the word, as the blessed James has written in his letter. 3. Are you worshipping the true God? 4. It is enough for her that she has done well. 5. That which I am writing is not for all of you. 6. We keep the festivals, supposing that we have them by God's commandment. 7. Next (ܐܬܗ) we write *memre* composed by Mar Ephrem. 8. I am not afraid of those who accuse me. 9. I suppose that you are the one about whom the prophets wrote. 10. O Lord (*lit.* my lord), you know everything; you know that I love you.

11. OTHER NOUNS WITH VARIABLE VOWELS

The pe'al active participle is an example of a noun with an invariable vowel in the first syllable. There are other such nouns, all inflected in a similar way:

a. nouns like the participle with a long vowel in the first syllable, e.g. ܢܘܼܟ̣ܠܐ.

b. nouns in which a short vowel is followed by a consonant that is doubled. The writing system in Syriac does not show doubled letters, and nouns of this type, like ܐܡܪܐ *'emmrā* 'lamb', are not readily distinguished at sight in the emphatic state from nouns like ܡܲܠܟܐ.

c. nouns in which the first syllable contains a short vowel followed by two consonants, e.g. ܡܲܫܟܢܐ 'tent'. Normally nouns of this type are formed by the prefixing of one or more letters to the original root (in this case ܫܟܢ).

Masculine nouns in all these three classes add a short vowel (normally *a*) on the syllable beginning with the second root letter just in the abs. and cstr. sing. (the same pattern as in the active participle, §10). This vowel also appears before the 1st sing. and 2nd and 3rd pl. suffixes. Examples are:

emph.	abs., cstr.	with suffixes
ܢܘܼܟ̣ܠܐ	ܢܘܼܟܠ	ܢܘܼܟܠܣ, ܢܘܼܟܠܗ, ܢܘܼܟܠܝ, ܢܘܼܟܠܟܘܢ, etc.
ܐܡܪܐ	ܐܡܪ	ܐܡܪܗܝ, ܐܡܪܗ, ܐܡܪܝ, ܐܡܪܟܘܢ, ܐܡܪܢ, etc.
ܡܲܫܟܢܐ	ܡܲܫܟܢ	ܡܲܫܟܢܘܗܝ, ܡܲܫܟܢܗ, ܡܲܫܟܢܝ, ܡܲܫܟܢܟܘܢ, etc.
ܡܲܪܡܪܐ	ܡܲܪܡܪ	ܡܲܪܡܪܗܝ, ܡܲܪܡܪܗ, ܡܲܪܡܪܝ, ܡܲܪܡܪܟܘܢ, etc.

Plural forms of these nouns do not exhibit the extra vowel, with or without suffixes; thus: ܢܽܘܟ݂ܠܳܐ, ܢܽܘܟ݂ܠܶܟ, ܢܽܘܟ݂ܠܶܗ, ܢܽܘܟ݂ܠܰܝܗܶܢ, etc.

Feminine nouns of this kind, that is, with an invariable vowel at the beginning, include words like ܐܰܪܡܰܠܬܳܐ 'widow', ܡܶܐܟ݂ܽܘܠܬܳܐ 'food', ܐܶܫܬܽܘܚܬܳܐ 'praise'. They are inflected like the feminine active participle in that the vowel on the second root letter disappears in all forms except the emphatic singular. Thus:

sing. emph.	abs.	cstr.	pl. emph.	abs.	cstr.
ܐܰܪܡܰܠܬܳܐ	ܐܰܪܡܠܳܐ	ܐܰܪܡܰܠܬ݁	ܐܰܪܡܠܳܬܳܐ	ܐܰܪܡܠܳܢ	ܐܰܪܡܠܳܬ݁
ܡܶܐܟ݂ܽܘܠܬܳܐ	ܡܶܐܟ݂ܠܳܐ	ܡܶܐܟ݂ܠܰܬ݁	ܡܶܐܟ݂ܠܳܬܳܐ	ܡܶܐܟ݂ܠܳܢ	ܡܶܐܟ݂ܠܳܬ݁
ܐܶܫܬܽܘܚܬܳܐ	ܐܶܫܬܳܚ	ܐܶܫܬܰܚܬ݁	ܐܶܫܬܳܚܳܬܳܐ	ܐܶܫܬܳܚܳܢ	ܐܶܫܬܳܚܳܬ݁

A quite separate class of feminine nouns with variable vowels are those nouns, for the most part abstract, that end in ‐ܽܘܬܳܐ or ‐ܺܝܬܳܐ, for example ܡܰܠܟ݁ܽܘܬܳܐ 'kingdom', ܨܶܒ݂ܽܘܬܳܐ 'thing', ܨܠܽܘܬܳܐ 'prayer', ܐܶܫܬܰܥܺܝܬܳܐ 'story'. The ܘ and ܝ in these endings are vowels (u, o, i) in the singular, but become consonants (w, y) in the plural. The result is the following paradigm:

	sing.			pl.		
emph.	abs.	cstr.	emph.	abs.	cstr.
ܡܰܠܟ݁ܽܘܬܳܐ	ܡܰܠܟ݁ܽܘ	ܡܰܠܟ݁ܽܘܬ݁	ܡܰܠܟ݁ܘܳܬܳܐ	ܡܰܠܟ݁ܘܳܢ	ܡܰܠܟ݁ܘܳܬ݁
ܨܶܒ݂ܽܘܬܳܐ	ܨܶܒ݂ܽܘ	ܨܶܒ݂ܽܘܬ݁	ܨܶܒ݂ܘܳܬܳܐ	ܨܶܒ݂ܘܳܢ	ܨܶܒ݂ܘܳܬ݁
ܨܠܽܘܬܳܐ	ܨܠܽܘ	ܨܠܽܘܬ݁	ܨܠܰܘܳܬܳܐ	ܨܠܰܘܳܢ	ܨܠܰܘܳܬ݁
ܐܶܫܬܰܥܺܝܬܳܐ	ܐܶܫܬܰܥܺܝ	ܐܶܫܬܰܥܺܝܬ݁	ܐܶܫܬܰܥܝܳܬܳܐ	ܐܶܫܬܰܥܝܳܢ	ܐܶܫܬܰܥܝܳܬ݁

Notice how in the plural the change of vocalization can produce a cluster of consonants that is then resolved by an extra vowel near the beginning of the word. This happens in different ways in ܨ̈ܒܘܳܬ݂ܳܐ and ܨ̈ܠܘܳܬ݂ܳܐ.

Suffixes are attached in the regular way to all these feminine nouns, starting from the emphatic form minus the ending ܬܳܐ-; for example, ܡܐܟ݂ܘܠܬܝ 'my food', ܨܠܘܳܬ݂ܗܘܢ 'their prayer'.

More prepositions. A few prepositions have vowels that vary when suffixes are attached. Among these are:

ܒܳܬܰܪ 'after'. This takes singular suffixes, and the second vowel ܰ disappears before all *except* ܝ, ܟܘܢ, ܟܝܢ, ܗܘܢ, ܗܝܢ. Thus: ܒܳܬܰܪܝ, ܒܳܬ݂ܪܳܟ݂, ܒܳܬ݂ܪܶܗ, ܒܳܬ݂ܪܰܢ, ܒܳܬܰܪܟܘܢ, ܒܳܬܰܪܟܶܝܢ etc.

ܠܘܩܒܰܠ 'against'. The word in this form takes the suffixes ܝ, ܟܘܢ, ܟܝܢ, ܗܘܢ, ܗܝܢ only, the other (singular) suffixes being attached to the form ܠܘܩܒܠ- ; thus ܠܘܩܒܳܠܝ, ܠܘܩܒܰܠܟܘܢ, ܠܘܩܒܠܶܗ, ܠܘܩܒܠܶܟ݂ܝ, ܠܘܩܒܠܳܟ݂, etc.

Some further prepositions that take 'plural' suffixes are: ܚܠܳܦ 'instead of, on behalf of'; and ܕܠܳܐ 'without'. Also, the expression ܒܰܠܚܘܕ 'alone' takes these suffixes, as in:

ܐܰܠܳܗܳܐ ܒܰܠܚܘܕܰܘܗܝ God alone.

Another group of prepositions may be mentioned here. These are actually adverbs followed by ܡܶܢ. They are:

ܠܥܶܠ ܡܶܢ	above	ܠܬܰܚܬ ܡܶܢ	below
ܠܒܰܪ ܡܶܢ	outside	ܠܓܰܘ ܡܶܢ	inside, within
ܣܛܰܪ ܡܶܢ	except, aside from.		

Vocabulary

Syriac	English	Syriac	English
ܡܰܠܟܘܬ݂ܳܐ	kingdom (f.)	ܐܰܪܡܰܠܬܳܐ	widow (f.)
ܣܠܩ	go up	ܣܢܝ݂ܬ݂ܳܐ	sin (f.)
ܡܰܥܡܘܕ݂ܝܬ݂ܳܐ	baptism (f.)	ܐܳܦ	also, even
ܛܘܪܳܐ	mountain	ܗܶܪܛܝܩܐ	heretic
ܡܶܐܟ݂ܘܠܬ݂ܳܐ	food (f.)	ܡܰܙܡܘܪܳܐ	psalm
ܐܶܠܳܐ	but	ܨܠܘܬ݂ܳܐ	prayer (f.)
ܥܰܦܪܳܐ	dust	ܢܣܰܒ	take, take away
ܡܰܫܟܢܳܐ	tent	ܬܶܫܒܘܚܬܳܐ	praise, hymn
ܝܰܘܡܳܐ	day (m.); abs. ܝܘܡ;	ܗܳܐ	behold
	pl. usu. ܝܰܘܡܳܬ݂ܳܐ	ܐܶܡܪܳܐ	lamb
ܩܰܠܝ݂ܠ	a little, a few	ܓܰܘܳܐ	the inside; cstr. ܓܰܘ
	(indeclinable)	ܟܳܗܢܳܐ	priest
ܐܶܫܬܰܥܝܳܐ	history, story (f.)	ܪܶܓ݂ܠܳܐ	foot (f.)

Exercises

Translate into English:

P 32

Translate into Syriac:

1. every priest; all the priests of God. 2. Christ is like us apart from sin. 3. After my baptism I went up on the mountain by myself. 4. There are many widows in the church. 5. All the kingdoms of the world have fallen and are as dust. 6. He has written letters to all the churches in the kingdom. 7. Praise (to) God, who kept the blessed one (on) that day without (ܘܠܐ) sin. 8. Behold the lamb of God, who takes away the sin of the world. 9. We have our tent in this world, but we have also a tent in heaven made by God. 10. We do not eat every (kind of) food. Some foods are within the law, and some foods are outside it.

12. MISCELLANEOUS AND IRREGULAR NOUNS

Two groups of nouns remain to be dealt with:

a. short nouns like ܐܒܐ, ܐܚܐ, ܚܡܐ, ܒܐ. Not all the absolute and construct forms of these nouns are attested. See the list of irregular nouns below.

b. adjectives ending in -ān and nouns in -ānā. The former is a large class, e.g. ܫܡܝܢ 'heavenly' (from ܫܡܝܐ); the latter include *nomina agentis* like ܡܠܦܢܐ 'teacher'. All these have feminine forms with a *yod*. For ܫܡܝܢ the feminine forms are: abs. ܫܡܝܢܐ, cstr. ܫܡܝܢܬ, emph. ܫܡܝܢܝܬܐ; pl. abs. ܫܡܝܢܝܢ, cstr. ܫܡܝܢܝܬ, emph. ܫܡܝܢܝܬܐ. Likewise, ܡܠܦܢܝܬܐ is 'female teacher'; pl. ܡܠܦܢܝܬܐ.

The following are the most important irregular nouns.

ܐܢܫ   'someone, one'. ܠܐ ܐܢܫ 'no one'. ܟܠ ܐܢܫ (or written together ܟܠܢܫ) 'everyone'.

ܐܢܫܐ   'people'. Formally this is the emphatic of ܐܢܫ but it is usually written with *seyame* and construed as plural, as in ܐܢܫܐ ܣܓܝܐܐ 'many people'. The absolute pl. ܐܢܫܝܢ, occurs in such phrases as ܐܢܫܝܢ ܐܡܪܝܢ 'people say'. There is also a construct ܐܢܫܝ. With suffixes e.g. ܐܢܫܘܗܝ 'his people'.

ܐܢܫܐ ܒܪ   'man, person'.[1] The abs. ܒܪ ܐܢܫ (or as one word, ܒܪܢܫ) is used in the same way as ܐܢܫ. There is a

---

[1] Never 'son of man'.

feminine ܒܰܪܰܬ݂ ܐ݈ܢܳܫܳܐ. Pl. ܒܢܰ̈ܝ ܐ݈ܢܳܫܳܐ (or ܒܰܪܢܳܫ̈ܳܐ) 'people'; fem. ܒܢܳ̈ܬ݂ ܐ݈ܢܳܫܳܐ.

ܐܰܒ݂ܳܐ 'father' (*aḇā*). With suffixes ܐܰܒ݂ܝ (*āḇ*), ܐܰܒ݂ܽܘܟ݂, ܐܰܒ݂ܽܘܟ݂ܝ, ܐܰܒ݂ܽܘܗ݈ܝ (*aḇu*), ܐܰܒ݂ܽܘܗ̇ (*aḇuh*), ܐܰܒ݂ܽܘܢ, ܐܰܒ݂ܽܘܟ݂ܽܘܢ, ܐܰܒ݂ܽܘܟ݂ܶܝܢ, ܐܰܒ݂ܽܘܗܽܘܢ, ܐܰܒ݂ܽܘܗܶܝܢ. There are two plurals, ܐܰܒ݂ܳܗ̈ܶܐ and ܐܰܒ݂ܳܗ̈ܳܬ݂ܳܐ, both masculine, but the latter takes suffixes like a feminine plural.

ܐܰܚܳܐ 'brother'. Inflected like ܐܰܒ݂ܳܐ in the singular; thus with suffixes ܐܰܚܝ, ܐܰܚܽܘܟ݂, etc. Pl. ܐܰܚܶ̈ܐ. Notice the pair of words ܐܰܚܽܘܗ݈ܝ / ܐܰܚ̈ܽܘܗ݈ܝ 'his brother'/ 'his brothers'.

ܚܳܬ݂ܳܐ 'sister'. With suffixes ܚܳܬ݂ܝ, ܚܳܬ݂ܳܟ݂, etc. Pl. ܐܰܚܘ̈ܳܬ݂ܳܐ.

ܐܶܡܳܐ 'mother'. Cstr. ܐܶܡ; with suffixes ܐܶܡܝ, ܐܶܡܳܟ݂, etc. Pl. ܐܶܡܗ̈ܳܬ݂ܳܐ.

ܒܪܳܐ 'son'. Cstr. ܒܰܪ; with suffixes ܒܶܪܝ, ܒܶܪܳܟ݂, ܒܶܪܶܟ݂ܝ, ܒܶܪܶܗ, ܒܶܪܳܗ̇, ܒܶܪܟ݂ܽܘܢ, ܒܶܪܟ݂ܶܝܢ, etc. Pl. emph. ܒܢܰ̈ܝܳܐ, abs. ܒܢܺ̈ܝܢ, cstr. ܒܢܰ̈ܝ. Words like this one having the emphatic plural in ܰܝܳܐ- (this is an older Aramaic ending) take suffixes as if the ending were the usual ܶܐ- : in this case, ܒܢܰ̈ܝ ('my sons'), ܒܢܰ̈ܘܗ݈ܝ, ܒܢܰ̈ܝܗ̇ etc.

ܒܰܪܬ݂ܳܐ 'daughter'. Cstr. ܒܰܪܰܬ݂ (*baṯ*); with suffixes ܒܰܪܬ݂ܝ, ܒܰܪܬ݂ܳܟ݂, ܒܰܪܬ݂ܟ݂ܽܘܢ, etc. Pl. ܒܢܳ̈ܬ݂ܳܐ; cstr. ܒܢܳ̈ܬ݂; with suffixes ܒܢܳ̈ܬ݂ܝ, ܒܢܳ̈ܬ݂ܳܟ݂, ܒܢܳ̈ܬ݂ܶܟ݂ܝ, etc.

ܐܰܢ̱ܬ݁ܬ݂ܳܐ 'woman, wife' (*atṯā* or *atā*). Cstr. ܐܰܢ̱ܬ݁ܰܬ݂. With suffixes ܐܰܢ̱ܬ݁ܬ݂ܝ, ܐܰܢ̱ܬ݁ܬ݂ܳܟ݂, ܐܰܢ̱ܬ݁ܬ݂ܶܗ, etc. Pl. ܢܶܫ̈ܶܐ; with suffixes ܢܶܫ̈ܰܝ, ܢܶܫ̈ܰܝܟ݂, etc.

ܫܡܐ   'name'. Abs. and cstr. ܫܶܡ; with suffixes ܫܶܡܝ, ܫܡܳܟ, ܫܡܗܘܢ, etc. Pl. ܫܡܳܗ̈ܶܐ or ܫܡܳܗ̈ܳܬܐ; the former with suffixes ܫܡܳܗܰܝ̈, etc.

ܐܚܪܺܝܢ   'other' (ḥrin). This is thoroughly irregular:

sing. abs.	emph.	cstr.	pl. abs.	emph.	cstr.
m. ܐܚܪܺܝܢ	ܐܚܪܺܢܐ	ܐܚܪܺܝܢ	ܐܚܪܳܢܺܝܢ	ܐܚܪ̈ܳܢܶܐ	ܐܚܪ̈ܳܢܰܝ
f. ܐܚܪܺܬܐ	ܐܚܪܳܝܬܐ	ܐܚܪܺܬ	ܐܚܪ̈ܳܢܝܳܢ	ܐܚܪ̈ܳܝܳܬܐ	ܐܚܪ̈ܳܝܳܬ

This word should not be confused with a different adjective ܐܚܪܳܝ (ḥrāy) 'latter, last'. 'The latter' (f.) is ܐܚܪܳܝܬܐ; 'the other' (f.) is ܐܚܪܺܬܐ.

ܒܰܝܬܐ   'house' (m.). Abs. (rare) ܒܰܝ; cstr. ܒܶܝܬ; with suffixes ܒܰܝܬܝ, ܒܰܝܬܟ, etc. Pl. ܒ̈ܳܬܐ.

ܩܪܺܝܬܐ   'village' (f.). Abs. ܩܪܳܐ; cstr. ܩܪܺܝܬ; with suffixes ܩܪܺܝܬܝ etc. Pl. ܩܘܪ̈ܝܐ; with suffixes usu. ܩܘܪ̈ܝ, ܩܘܪ̈ܝܟ, ܩܘܪ̈ܝܗ, etc.

ܐܺܝܕܐ   'hand' (f.). Cstr. ܐܺܝܕ. Pl. ܐܺܝܕ̈ܝܢ or ܐܺܝܕ̈ܐ. The combination ܒܝܕ or ܒܐܺܝܕ (lit. 'by the hand(s) of') means generally 'by means of, through'. This can take suffixes, e.g. ܒܐܺܝܕܰܝ̈ܗܘܢ 'through them'.

ܙܢܐ   'kind, type'. Abs. ܙܢ. The abs. pl. occurs in the phrase ܙܢܺܝ̈ܢ ܙܢܺܝ̈ܢ 'various kinds'. Emph. pl. ܙܢ̈ܰܝܐ. Similarly inflected are ܕܡܐ 'blood' (with suffixes ܕܡܝ, ܕܡܟ, etc.); and ܚܕܝܐ 'breast' (pl. ܚܕܰܝ̈ܐ).

ܫܢܬܐ   'year' (f.). Abs. ܫܢܐ; cstr. ܫܢܰܬ. Pl. ܫܢ̈ܰܝܐ; abs. ܫܢܺܝ̈ܢ; cstr. ܫܢܰܝ̈; with suffixes ܫܢܰܝ̈, ܫܢܰܝ̈ܟ, etc.

ܫܡܝܐ 'heaven'. Usually construed as singular, but like a plural in its inflection; thus abs. ܫܡܝܢ, cstr. ܫܡܝ.

Vocabulary

ܦܩܕ	command, bid	ܫܒܩ	leave, dismiss, allow, forgive
ܫܦܪ	be pleasing	ܢܩܦ	cling, adhere, cleave, follow
ܐܡܝܢ	amen	ܥܘܕܪܢܐ	help
ܗܟܢܐ	thus	ܫܡܝܢܝ	heavenly
ܥܕܬܢܝ	ecclesiastical	ܕܒܚܬܐ	sacrifice (*f.*)
ܐܝܟܢܐ	how, as	ܨܒܘܬܐ	thing, matter (*f.*)
ܒܪܫܝܬ	in the beginning; Genesis	ܪܘܚܐ ܕܩܘܕܫܐ	Holy Spirit (*usually m.*)
ܝܘܚܢܢ	John		
ܕܡܐ	blood		

Exercises

Translate into English:

1. ܫܡܥܢ ܗܟܢܐ ܒܟܬܒܐ ܕܒܪܫܝܬ: ܕܐܢܬܬܐ ܡܢ ܓܒܪܐ ܢܣܝܒܐ. ܡܛܠ ܗܢܐ ܢܫܒܘܩ ܓܒܪܐ ܠܐܒܘܗܝ ܘܠܐܡܗ ܘܢܩܦ ܠܐܢܬܬܗ.
2. ܥܡ ܥܘܕܪܢܐ ܕܡܪܢ ܫܠܡܬ݀ ܐܟܬܒܬܐ ܠܟܠܗܘܢ ܟܬܒܐ ܥܕܬܢܝܐ.
3. ܐܝܬ ܠܝ ܦܘܪܩܢܐ ܠܐ ܒܕܡܐ ܕܕܒܚܬܐ ܐܠܐ ܒܝܕ ܗܝܡܢܘܬܐ ܒܕܡܗ ܕܡܫܝܚܐ.
4. ܒܬܪ ܬܘܕܝܬܐ ܡܛܠ ܫܒܩ ܡܢ ܐܡܝ ܠܓܒܪܐ ܚܛܝܐ ܘܥܘܠܐ ܚܛܝܬܐ.
5. ܡܥܡܘܕܝܬܐ ܟܪܣܛܝܢܝܬܐ ܐܝܬܝܗ ܒܫܡ ܐܒܐ ܘܒܪܐ ܘܪܘܚܐ ܕܩܘܕܫܐ.
6. ܓܒܪܐ: ܠܐ ܐܒܘܗܝ ܐܝܬܝ ܐܠܐ ܚܕ ܒܢܝ ܐܢܫܐ ܐܝܟ ܐܒܘܟܘܢ.

7. لُلْ هُلُا نُمِعُه ܘܦܪܝܫܐ ܗܢܘܟܐܗ : ܘܐܢܬܘܐܐܗ ܘܐܣܩܘܗܝ ܟܟܝ /ܠܢܩܢ
Translate into Syriac:

1. She took a little of her brother's food.   2. We have kept the faith of our fathers and mothers.   3. God is wiser than men.   4. We know the name of their mother, and their father is in our village.   5. The blessed one went up by himself as his parents (*lit.* fathers) commanded.   6. There is no other gospel than (*lit.* aside from) the one that we heard from the apostles.   7. My daughter, it is well that your sons and your daughters cleave to you.   8. I suppose that others have not heard about this matter.   9. Our heavenly father knows what food is enough for us.   10. In all their houses there is no one who has a Psalter (*lit.* book of Psalms).

13. THE IMPERFECT TENSE

The imperfect tense is primarily future in meaning, but it also functions in purpose clauses, negative imperatives, and jussives.

Inflection. The imperfect is inflected by a combination of preformatives and afformatives. The paradigm for ܩܛܠ is:

	sing.		pl.	
3rd m.	ܢܶܩܛܽܘܠ	he will kill	ܢܶܩܛܠܽܘܢ	they will kill
3rd f.	ܬܶܩܛܽܘܠ	she will kill	ܢܶܩܛܠܳܢ	they will kill
2nd m.	ܬܶܩܛܽܘܠ	you will kill	ܬܶܩܛܠܽܘܢ	you will kill
2nd f.	ܬܶܩܛܠܺܝܢ	you will kill	ܬܶܩܛܠܳܢ	you will kill
1st	ܐܶܩܛܽܘܠ	I will kill	ܢܶܩܛܽܘܠ	we will kill.

(margin note: O is short here)

Notice that in those forms that have no afformative, a vowel appears between the second and third root letters. In the case of ܩܛܠ this vowel is *o*. Other cases will appear below.

If the second root letter is a *bgdkpt*, it has the hard pronunciation. Thus, for the verb ܟܬܒ the impf. is ܢܶܟܬܽܘܒ.

For the 3rd feminine singular there is another (West Syriac only) form with a *yod* at the end, e.g. ܬܶܩܛܠܺܝܢ, which distinguishes it in writing (but not pronunciation) from the 2nd masculine.

All the fem. pl. forms of the impf. are written with *seyame*.

The stem vowel in the impf. may be *o*, *a* or *e*. In general, those mostly transitive verbs that have the vowel *a* in the perfect have *o* in the imperfect, as with ܩܛܠ above. Verbs that have the vowel *e* in the perfect normally have *a* in the imperfect, e.g. ܕܚܶܠ (pf.) / ܢܶܕܚܰܠ (impf.). Exceptions are:

a. some verbs that have *a* in both perfect and imperfect. These include most verbs with a guttural or ܪ as the third root letter, e.g. ܫܡܰܥ/ܢܶܫܡܰܥ, ܥܒܰܪ/ܢܶܥܒܰܪ; and a few others, e.g. ܫܠܶܛ/ܢܶܫܠܰܛ ('have authority').

b. the verbs ܥܒܰܕ/ܢܶܥܒܶܕ and ܙܒܰܢ/ܢܶܙܒܶܢ ('buy'), which have *a* in the perfect and *e* in the imperfect.

c. a few verbs that have *e* in the perfect and *o* in the imperfect, the most important of which are ܣܓܶܕ/ܢܶܣܓܽܘܕ, ܫܬܶܩ/ܢܶܫܬܽܘܩ ('be silent'), and ܩܪܶܒ/ܢܶܩܪܽܘܒ.

The paradigm for verbs with impf. in *a* and *e* is as follows:

	in *a*: sing.	pl.	in *e*: sing.	pl.
3rd m.	ܢܶܕܚܰܠ	ܢܶܕܚܠܽܘܢ	ܢܶܥܒܶܕ	ܢܶܥܒܕܽܘܢ
3rd f.	ܬܶܕܚܰܠ	ܢܶܕܚܠܳܢ	ܬܶܥܒܶܕ	ܢܶܥܒܕܳܢ
2nd m.	ܬܶܕܚܰܠ	ܬܶܕܚܠܽܘܢ	ܬܶܥܒܶܕ	ܬܶܥܒܕܽܘܢ
2nd f.	ܬܶܕܚܠܺܝܢ	ܬܶܕܚܠܳܢ	ܬܶܥܒܕܺܝܢ	ܬܶܥܒܕܳܢ
1st	ܐܶܕܚܰܠ	ܢܶܕܚܰܠ	ܐܶܥܒܶܕ	ܢܶܥܒܶܕ

Usage. The imperfect is used for indicating an action that is incomplete or in the future. In a subordinate clause, the future is relative to the main clause. Thus:

ܣܶܠܩܰܬ ܕܬܶܣܓܽܘܕ she went up to worship (*lit*. that she might worship).

A clause expressing purpose, as in this example, can be introduced more explicitly by ܐܰܝܟ ܕ- or ܐܰܝܟܰܢܳܐ ܕ- 'in order that':

ܟܬܰܒܢ ܠܶܐܓܰܪܬܳܐ ܐܰܝܟܰܢܳܐ ܕܬܶܫܡܥܽܘܢ ܫܪܳܪܳܐ We wrote the letter so that you might hear the truth.

The negative is ܘܲܕܠܡܳܐ ܢܩܘܡ 'lest', as in: ܐܢ̈ܫܝ ܢܥܩ̈ܗܝܢܠܠܐ ܘܲܕܠܡܳܐ ܢܩܘܡ 'the women fled lest he should kill them'.

The imperative (§14) is not used with ܠܐ, and the imperfect is the only way to express a prohibition. Thus:

<blockquote>

ܠܐ ܬܩܛܘܠ   thou shalt not kill

ܠܐ ܬܕܚܠܝ ܡܪܝܡ   do not be afraid, Mary.

</blockquote>

The imperfect also expresses the jussive ('let …'), as in:

<blockquote>

ܢܬܩܪܒ ܠܗܝܟܠܐ   let us draw near to the temple.

</blockquote>

Vocabulary[1]

ܛܥܡ	taste, *a*	ܙܒܢ	buy, *e*
ܙܡܪ	sing, *a*	ܦܪܫ	separate, *o*
ܥܡܪ	dwell, *a*	ܛܒܐ or ܛܒܐ	news, report
ܠܚܡܐ	bread	ܝܬܝܪܐܝܬ	especially
ܡܟܝܢ	lawful, *authorized*	ܫܒܬܐ	week, sabbath (*f.*)
ܥܒܕܐ	thing, deed	ܥܕ ܠܐ	while; ܥܕ ܠܐ before
ܥܡܐ	people, nation; *Jews*	ܥܕܡܐ	until (+-ܠ or -ܘ)
pl. ܥܡ̈ܡܐ *Gentiles*		ܡܘܬܐ	death
ܘܲܕܠܡܳܐ	lest, perhaps	ܐܝܟܐ	where

Exercises

Translate into English:

1. ܠܐ ܗܘܐ ܘܒܝܢ ܫܪܐܘܟܬܐ܆ ܐܠܐ ܡܟܝܠ ܠܚܡܐ.

2. ܚܙܘ ܥܡܐ ܐܝܟ ܘܟܥܬܒܠܟܐ ܐܝܢ ܢܕܚܘܢ ܠܗܝܟܠܐ.

---

[1] From now on, the vowel of the imperfect is given for each verb used in the pe'al.

Translate into Syriac:

1. Some say it is not lawful for a man to divorce his wife.
2. How shall we sing to the Lord in a land that is not ours?
3. Do not do this evil thing, my sister.   4. Let this story that we shall write be pleasing to God.   5. We will not be afraid as long as (*lit.* while) we have the blessing of the saint (*f.*).   6. The women went up to the city to buy food for themselves (*use* ܢܦܫܗ).   7. By the grace of God we shall taste the fruits of the land.   8. Let them do as I have commanded.   9. My brother, I have a little time and I shall write this letter to you and to our sister.   10. Other gods, the gods of the Gentiles (*lit.* nations), you (*m. sing.*) shall not worship.

14. THE IMPERATIVE AND INFINITIVE. THE VERB ܗܘܳܐ

The imperative. The masculine singular of the imperative is formed from the imperfect by dropping the preformative. The other forms, masculine plural and feminine singular and plural, are then made by adding endings. For the various classes of verb we have:

(perfect)		ܩܛܰܠ	ܕܚܶܠ	ܥܒܰܕ
(imperfect)		ܢܶܩܛܘܿܠ	ܢܶܕܚܰܠ	ܢܶܥܒܶܕ
imperative	m. sing.	ܩܛܘܿܠ	ܕܚܰܠ	ܥܒܶܕ
	f. sing.	ܩܛܘܿܠܝ	ܕܚܰܠܝ	ܥܒܶܕܝ
	m. pl.	ܩܛܘܿܠܘ	ܕܚܰܠܘ	ܥܒܶܕܘ
	f. pl.	ܩܛܘܿܠܝ̈	ܕܚܰܠܝ̈	ܥܒܶܕܝ̈

The endings are silent: all these forms are pronounced *qṭol* or *dḥal* or *ʿbed*. There are, however, longer forms of the plural which do distinguish it in pronunciation:

m. pl.	ܩܛܘܿܠܘܿܢ	ܕܚܰܠܘܿܢ	ܥܒܶܕܘܿܢ
f. pl.	ܩܛܘܿܠܶܝ̈ܢ	ܕܚܰܠܶܝ̈ܢ	ܥܒܶܕܶܝ̈ܢ

Notice that *seyame* points go on all feminine plural forms.

The meaning of the imperative is straightforward: ܟܬܘܿܒ, ܟܬܘܿܒܝ, etc. 'write!'. (Remember that the negative imperative is expressed by the imperfect: ܠܳܐ ܬܶܟܬܘܿܒ, ܠܳܐ ܬܶܟܬܒܺܝܢ, etc. 'do not write!'.)

The infinitive. All infinitives in Syriac begin with ܡ-. The infinitive peʿal is ܡܶܩܛܰܠ. The vowel on the second root letter is always *a* irrespective of the stem vowel in the perfect or imperfect. If the second root letter is a *bgdkpt*, it takes *qushaya*, e.g. ܡܸܟܬܲܒ݂ 'to write'.

The infinitive is prefixed with ܠ-, somewhat like the 'to' of the infinitive in English. Examples are:

ܣܶܠܩܲܬ݂ ܠܡܸܣܓܲܕ݂	she went up to worship
ܦܰܐܝܵܐ ܠܝܼ ܠܲܡܙܲܡܵܪܘ	it is fitting for me to sing
ܠܵܐ ܪܸܚܠܘ ܗ݂ܘܲܘ ܘܲܠܡܸܟ݂ܬܲܒ݂	they were not afraid of writing
ܐܝܼܬ݂ ܠܲܢ ܠܡܸܫܡܲܥ	it is for us to listen – we have to listen (*or* we can listen)

Syriac also has an 'infinitive absolute'. In this construction the infinitive, without ܠ-, goes alongside (usually before) a verb or participle for emphasis; e.g.

ܡܸܫܬܲܩ ܫܬܸܩܘ	they were completely silent
ܡܸܦܩܲܕ݂ ܦܵܩܕ݂ܝܼܢܲܢ ܠܟ݂ܘܿܢ	we strictly command you.

The verb ܗܘܵܐ. The verb ܗܘܵܐ 'be' will be met in §26, but it is helpful to learn now the pe'al perfect in its enclitic form. The conjugation is as follows, with pronunciations. As indicated by the *linea occultans*, the initial consonant ܗ is silent throughout.

	singular		plural	
3rd m.	ܗܘܵܐ	*wā*	ܗ݂ܘܲܘ	*waw*
3rd f.	ܗܘܵܬ݂	*wāṯ*	ܗܘܲܝ	*wāy*
2nd m.	ܗܘܲܝܬ݂	*wayt*	ܗܘܲܝܬܘܿܢ	*wayton*
2nd f.	ܗܘܲܝܬܝ	*wayt*	ܗܘܲܝܬܹܝܢ	*wayten*
1st	ܗܘܝܼܬ݂	*wiṯ*	ܗܘܲܝܢ	*wayn.*

The verb in this enclitic form coming after (not before) a participle, adjective, or noun has the meaning 'was/were'. After ܗܘܐ it likewise puts the meaning of the expression into the past. Thus:

ܟܬܒܝܢ ܗܘܝܢ	we were writing
ܝܫܘܥ ܫܬܝܩ ܗܘܐ	Jesus was silent
ܓܒܪܐ ܟܘܡܪܐ ܗܘܐ	the man was a priest
ܡܝܐ ܐܝܬ ܗܘܐ ܠܗܘܢ	they had water
ܘܐܪܡܠܬܐ ܐܝܟܡܬܝ ܗܘܝ	they were widows.

ܗܘܐ can also appear after finite verbs, pf. and impf., and occasionally elsewhere in a sentence, but in these constructions it is almost meaningless. After a pf., it may put the action further into the past; e.g., ܣܠܩ ܗܘܐ ܕܝܢ ܐܦ ܝܘܣܦ 'Joseph too went (or had gone) up'. But, as in this example,[1] the pluperfect sense is often hard to detect.

Vocabulary

ܫܬܩ	be silent, o	ܐܘܡܢ, ܐܘܢ	(ptcs. of ܐܘܢ) right
ܪܘܓܙܐ	anger, wrath	ܐܘܟܢܘܬܐ	righteousness (f.)
ܐܕܢܐ	time; abs. ܥܕܢ	ܐܝܠܢܐ	tree
ܢܟܫܐ, ܕܠܐ	(ptcs. of ܟܫܐ) fitting	ܐܢ	if
ܐܝܣܪܐܝܠ	Israel	ܙܒܢܐ	time, season,
ܐܢܫ	human (adj.)		moment
ܩܪܒܐ	war, battle	ܐܠܩܢܐ	Elkanah[2]
ܚܝܠܐ	force, power,	ܫܝܠܐ	Shiloh
	mighty work	ܩܐܝܢ	Cain

---

[1] Luke 2: 4. [2] I Sam 1: 1-3.

Exercises

Translate into English:

Translate into Syriac:

1. We were singing hymns. 2. There were other women with him. 3. All her sons were priests. 4. It is right to worship God alone. 5. Draw near and take (use ܢܣܒ) this letter that I have written. 6. The fruit was beautiful, but she was afraid to taste. 7. The sacrifice of Cain was not pleasing to God. 8. Forgive us as we have forgiven others. 9. If one city will not listen to your doctrine, flee to another. 10. There was a village there in which people were dwelling who had fled from the war.

15. THE ETHPEᶜEL

The ethpeᶜel is formed from the peᶜal by using the preformative ‑ܐܬ. This preformative has counterparts in other Semitic languages, where it has a reflexive meaning (as in 'he
hurt himself'). In Syriac, however, forms with ‑ܐܬ took
over the function of the passive (as in 'he was hurt'). The
ethpeᶜel is thus primarily the passive of the peᶜal.

Inflection. The ethpeᶜel perfect ('he was killed', etc.) is:

	sing.	pl.
3rd m.	ܐܬܩܛܠ	ܐܬܩܛܠܘ
3rd f.	ܐܬܩܲܛܠܬ	ܐܬܩܛܠܝ (ܐܬܩܛܠ)
2nd m.	ܐܬܩܛܠܬ	ܐܬܩܛܠܬܘܢ
2nd f.	ܐܬܩܛܠܬܝ	ܐܬܩܛܠܬܝܢ
1st	ܐܬܩܲܛܠܬ	ܐܬܩܛܠܢ

Notice that in the 1st sing. and the 3rd f. sing. the vowel on
the first root letter is *a*. Just as in the peᶜal, if the third
radical is a *bgdkpt*, it takes *qushaya* in the 3rd f. and 1st sing;
e.g., ܐܬܟܬܒܬ. There are the same longer forms for the 1st
pl. ܐܬܩܛܠܢܢ, and the 3rd m. and f. pl. ܐܬܩܛܠܘܢ and ܐܬܩܛܠܝܢ.

The imperfect ('he will be killed' etc.) is as follows:

	sing.	pl.
3rd m.	ܢܬܩܛܠ	ܢܬܩܛܠܘܢ
3rd f.	ܬܬܩܛܠ (ܬܬܩܛܠ)	ܢܬܩܛܠܢ
2nd m.	ܬܬܩܛܠ	ܬܬܩܛܠܘܢ
2nd f.	ܬܬܩܛܠܝܢ	ܬܬܩܛܠܢ
1st	ܐܬܩܛܠ	ܢܬܩܛܠ

In the imperative, the vowel unexpectedly shifts to the first
radical, and is *a*. The second radical may disappear in pronunciation and have *linea occultans* written below it. Thus:

m. sing.	ܐܶܬ݂ܩܰܛܶܠ	or	ܐܶܬ݂ܩܰܛܶܠ
f. sing.	ܐܶܬ݂ܩܰܛܶܠܝ	or	ܐܶܬ݂ܩܰܛܶܠܝ
m. pl.	ܐܶܬ݂ܩܰܛܶܠܘ	or	ܐܶܬ݂ܩܰܛܶܠܘ
f. pl.	ܐܶܬ݂ܩܰܛܶܠܝܢ	or	ܐܶܬ݂ܩܰܛܶܠܝܢ

All these forms are pronounced *etqaṭl* or *etqal*. As in the
peʿal there are also longer forms of the plural, ܐܶܬ݂ܩܰܛܶܠܘܢ (m.)
and ܐܶܬ݂ܩܰܛܶܠܝܢ (f.).

All participles except the peʿal have the preformative ـܡ.
That of the ethpeʿel (there is only one) is

ܡܶܬ݂ܩܛܶܠ   being killed.

This is inflected like other nouns with an invariable vowel
in the first syllable (§11). The plural is then ܡܶܬ݂ܩܰܛܠܝܢ, the
feminine ܡܶܬ݂ܩܰܛܠܐ, etc.

If the last root letter of a verb is a guttural or ܪ, the vowel
just before it (in various parts of the pf., impf., and ptcs.) is
a instead of *e*, as in ܐܶܬ݂ܢܛܰܪ (not ܐܶܬ݂ܢܛܶܪ) 'he was kept'.

The infinitive follows a pattern that will appear in all the
other conjugations (that is, all but the peʿal), with the two
final vowels *ā - u*. For the ethpeʿel it is

ܡܶܬ݂ܩܛܳܠܘ   to be killed.

If a verb stem begins with any of the letters ܬ ܕ ܛ ܣ ܨ , this
letter changes places with the ܬ of the ethpeʿel preformative.
In the case of ܕ or ܨ there is a further change and the ܬ
becomes ܕ or ܛ respectively. Thus, from ܣܒܰܠ we have

ܐܬܢܣܒ 'it was taken' (not ܐܢܬܣܒ). Other examples of this transposition and change are:

ܢܙܕܒܢ let it be bought (*not* ܢܬܕܒܢ *or even* ܢܬܙܒܢ)

ܡܨܛܠܒܘ to be crucified (*not* ܡܨܬܠܒܘ *or* ܡܬܨܠܒܘ).

Meaning. The meaning of the ethpeʿel can usually be inferred from the peʿal, but not always. For example, ܥܡܕ and ܐܬܥܡܕ both mean 'be baptized' (but the ethpeʿel form is the more common). Some verbs in the ethpeʿel do not occur in the peʿal, for example ܐܬܟܪܟ 'go around'. Other ethpeʿels have particular meanings, e.g., ܐܫܬܡܥ (from ܫܡܥ) 'obey'. The vocabularies will signal verbs like these as they are met.

Usage. With the ethpeʿel the logical subject of the action is introduced by ܡܢ (rather than ـܠ as with the passive participle); e.g.,

ܐܬܦܩܕ ܡܢ ܫܠܝܚܐ   it was commanded by the apostle.

Vocabulary

ܥܡܕ	*pe.* (*a*), *ethp.* be baptized	ܫܡܥ	*ethp.* obey
ܢܛܪ	*ethp.* take care (+ـܕ of), guard (+ ܡܢ against)	ܫܠܡ	be finished, *a*
		ܟܪܟ	*ethp.* go around
ܕܒܪ	lead, *a*	ܙܢܐ	form, fashion, *o*
ܨܠܒ	crucify, *o* *raise up stake*	ܐܦܣܩܘܦܐ	bishop
ܚܫܒ	reckon, *o*	ܚܛܝܬܐ	sin
ܓܘܕܦܐ	blasphemy	ܐܣܛܪܛܝܘܛܐ	soldier
ܝܘܡܢܐ	today	ܕܘܟܬܐ (*m.*) or ܕܘܟܐ (*f.*) place
ܛܠܝܐ	child; *pl. usu.* ܛܠܝܐ, *f.* ܛܠܝܬܐ, *pl.* ܛܠܝܬܐ	ܠܘܩܕܡ	first, beforehand
		ܐܒܪܗܡ	Abraham
		ܦܬܟܪܐ	idol

Exercises

Translate into English:

Translate into Syriac:

1. You have been reckoned the people (*lit.* sons) of the kingdom.   2. Children, obey your parents in the Lord. 3. It is fitting for me to be baptized by you.   4. Take care lest you be led into unfaith (*lit.* not faith).   5. Heaven and earth were formed first, and after them we were formed. 6. For the sake of my name you shall be led before kings

---

[1] ܣܟܚܐ is naturally masculine in this context. (Why?)

and be accounted evildoers.　　7. To women the bishop says in his letter, Your sins shall be forgiven.　　8. Abraham's faith was reckoned to him for righteousness.　　9. From there Jesus was led by the soldiers to a (certain) place to be crucified.　　10. You were no longer allowed (*use* ܐܫܟܚ) to worship idols formed by human hands.

16. THE PAᶜEL AND ETHPAᶜAL

The paᶜel and its passive the ethpaᶜal are formally known as 'intensive' conjugations – expressing, that is, a stronger or repeated sense compared to the peᶜal. (This description, however, turns out to fit these conjugations in Syriac only very incompletely: see p. 75.)

Inflection. In the paᶜel and ethpaᶜal the second letter of the verb stem is doubled. This doubling is not seen or pro-nounced except when that letter is a *bgdkpt*, in which case it takes *qushaya*; or when the third letter is a *bgdkpt*, in which case it takes *rukaka* after the doubled second letter. (Ex-amples of these cases are given below.)

In the paᶜel, the preformatives and afformatives are the same as in the peᶜal. The vowel *a* remains on the first radi-cal throughout the conjugation. The preformatives for the imperfect, participles, and infinitive have no vowel (except for the *alaph* of the 1st sing. impf., which must have one). The paradigm is as follows:

perfect	sing.	pl.
3rd m.	ܩܰܛܶܠ	ܩܰܛܶܠܘ or ܩܰܛܶܠܘܢ
3rd f.	ܩܰܛܠܰܬ	ܩܰܛܶܠ (ܩܰܛܶܠܝܢ) or ܩܰܛܶܠܝ
2nd m.	ܩܰܛܶܠܬ	ܩܰܛܶܠܬܘܢ
2nd f.	ܩܰܛܶܠܬܝ	ܩܰܛܶܠܬܝܢ
1st	ܩܰܛܠܶܬ	ܩܰܛܶܠܢ or ܩܰܛܶܠܢܢ

imperfect	sing.	pl.
3rd m.	ܢܩܛܠ	ܢܩܛܠܘܢ
3rd f.	ܬܩܛܠ (ܢܩܛܠܢ)	ܢܩܛܠܢ
2nd m.	ܬܩܛܠ	ܬܩܛܠܘܢ
2nd f.	ܬܩܛܠܝܢ	ܬܩܛܠܢ
1st	ܐܩܛܠ	ܢܩܛܠ

imperative		
masc.	ܩܛܠ	ܩܛܠܘ or ܩܛܠܘܢ
fem.	ܩܛܠܝ	ܩܛܠܝܢ or ܩܛܠܝܢ

participles:

active   ܡܩܛܠ (f. ܡܩܛܠܐ, f. emph. ܡܩܛܠܬܐ, etc.)

passive   ܡܩܛܠ (f. ܡܩܛܠܐ, f. emph. ܡܩܛܠܬܐ, etc.)

infinitive: ܡܩܛܠܘ

If the third radical of a verb is a guttural or ܪ, the *e* vowel before it becomes *a*; e.g., ܫܕܪ 'send', impf. ܢܫܕܪ, ptc. ܡܫܕܪ, etc.

A *nomen agentis* in the paʿel has the form ܡܩܛܠܢܐ 'killer'. This form occurs as an adjective also, e.g. ܡܪܚܡܢ 'showing mercy – merciful'.

For the ethpaʿal the paradigm is:

perfect	sing.	pl.
3rd m.	ܐܬܩܛܠ	ܐܬܩܛܠܘ or ܐܬܩܛܠܘܢ
3rd f.	ܐܬܩܛܠܬ	ܐܬܩܛܠܝ (ܐܬܩܛܠܢ) or ܐܬܩܛܠܐ
2nd m.	ܐܬܩܛܠܬ	ܐܬܩܛܠܬܘܢ
2nd f.	ܐܬܩܛܠܬܝ	ܐܬܩܛܠܬܝܢ
1st	ܐܬܩܛܠܬ	ܐܬܩܛܠܢ or ܐܬܩܛܠܢܢ

imperfect	sing.	pl.
3rd m.	ܢܡܩܗܠ	ܢܡܩܗܠܢ
3rd f.	ܬܡܩܗܠ (ܐܬܡܩܗܠ)	ܢܡܩܗܠܢ
2nd m.	ܐܬܡܩܗܠ	ܐܬܡܩܗܠܢ
2nd f.	ܐܬܡܩܗܠܝܢ	ܐܬܡܩܗܠܢ
1st	ܐܬܡܩܗܠ	ܢܡܩܗܠ

imperative:

| masc. | ܐܬܡܩܗܠ | ܐܬܡܩܗܠܘ or ܐܬܡܩܗܠܢ |
| fem. | ܐܬܡܩܗܠܝ | ܐܬܡܩܗܠܝܢ or ܐܬܡܩܗܠܢ |

(There are also forms ܐܬܩܗܠܝ *etqal* etc.)

participle: ܡܬܡܩܗܠ

infinitive: ܡܬܡܩܗܠܘ

In the ethpa'al, initial ܘ ܡ ܪ ܗ change places with the ܬ of the preformative, just as in the ethpe'el.

Examples of verbs with *bgdkpt* letters are ܩܒܠ 'receive', in which the ܒ is doubled throughout; and ܩܪܒ 'offer', in which the ܒ is pronounced soft after the doubled ܪ in forms like ܩܪܒܬ 'I offered' and ܐܬܩܪܒܬ 'it (*f.*) was offered'.

Usage and meaning. Verbs in the pa'el can be classified as follows.

a. A minority of verbs actually exhibit the difference set out at the beginning of this lesson, that the pa'el is an intensified pe'al. ܩܛܠ is one of these; hence ܩܛܠ 'slay many'. Another is ܢܫܩ 'kiss' – ܢܫܩ 'cover with kisses'. Just as often, a verb is used in both pe'al and pa'el without much difference in meaning, e.g. ܥܕܰܪ and ܥܰܕܰܪ 'help'; ܦܩܰܕ and ܦܰܩܶܕ 'command'; ܙܡܰܪ and ܙܰܡܰܪ 'sing'.

b. The paʿel may make the peʿal transitive, as with ܦܚܰܡ 'be comparable' – ܦܰܚܶܡ 'compare'.

c. Some verbs have a new meaning in the paʿel, for example ܩܰܪܶܒ 'offer, present'.

d. A number of verbs occur in the paʿel but not the peʿal. Examples include several in the vocabulary on the next page, e.g. ܥܰܕܰܪ and ܡܰܠܶܠ.

e. A special class of these paʿel-only verbs are the 'denominative' verbs, formed by putting the vowels of the paʿel onto a noun. Examples are ܚܰܝܶܠ 'strengthen' (from ܚܰܝܠܳܐ) and ܠܰܒܶܒ 'encourage' (from ܠܶܒܳܐ *lebba*).

The verb ܩܰܕܶܡ is used in front of another verb, without *waw* intervening, to give the sense of 'beforehand', as in

ܩܰܕܶܡܘ ܡܰܠܶܠܘ ܢܒܺܝ̈ܶܐ ܥܰܠ ܗܳܕܶܐ the prophets spoke beforehand about this.

Quadriliteral verbs. Some verb stems have four letters. These verbs may be denominative, e.g. ܬܰܠܡܶܕ 'evangelize' (from ܬܰܠܡܺܝܕܳܐ),[1] or loan-words, e.g. ܩܰܛܪܶܓ 'accuse' (from Greek *κατηγορεῖν*). They are conjugated like paʿels in which instead of a doubled middle root letter there are two different single letters. Thus for ܬܰܠܡܶܕ we have

pf. ܬܰܠܡܶܕ, ܬܰܠܡܕܰܬ, ܬܰܠܡܶܕܬ, ܬܰܠܡܶܕܬܽܘܢ, etc.

[1] In dictionaries this verb is apt to be treated as a taphʿel conjugation of ܠܡܕ. See pp. 81-2.

impf. ܢܣܰܒܰܪ, ܐܶܣܰܒܰܪ, ܢܣܰܒܪܽܘܢ, etc.; imv. ܣܰܒܰܪ etc.
participles ܡܣܰܒܰܪ, ܡܣܰܒܱܪ ; infinitive ܡܣܰܒܳܪܽܘ
ethpaʿal ܐܶܬ݂ܣܰܒܰܪ, ܢܶܬ݂ܣܰܒܰܪ, ܡܶܬ݂ܣܰܒܰܪ, ܡܶܬ݂ܣܰܒܳܪܽܘ.

Vocabulary

ܫܰܕܰܪ	*pa.* send	ܩܰܒܶܠ	*pa.* receive
ܩܰܪܶܒ	*pa.* offer	ܣܰܒܰܪ	evangelize
ܦܰܫܶܩ	*pa.* expound	ܓܰܕܶܦ	*pa.* blaspheme
ܩܰܕܶܡ	*pa.* do beforehand	ܝܰܩܰܪ	*pa.* honour
ܠܰܒܶܒ[2]	encourage	ܚܰܝܶܠ	*pa.* strengthen
ܫܰܒܰܚ	*pa.* glorify	ܡܰܠܶܠ[2]	*pa.* speak
ܗܰܝܡܶܢ	believe	ܗܰܠܶܟ	*pa.* walk
ܐܰܘ	or	ܚܳܣ	far be it!
ܐܽܘܪܚܳܐ	way, road (*f.*)	ܕܺܝܢܳܐ	judgement
ܡܶܚܕܳܐ	at once	ܐܰܬ݂ܪܳܐ	place (*m.*); *pl.* ܐܰܬ݂ܪ̈ܘܳܬ݂ܳܐ
ܪܰܚܶܡ	*pa.*, *ethpa.* have mercy (+ܥܰܠ on)		

Exercises

Translate into English:

1. ܩܰܕܶܡ ܦܰܩܶܕ ܠܗܽܘܢ ܐܰܝܟ ܕܢܰܠܦܽܘܢ ܐܶܢܽܘܢ.
2. ܡܳܢܳܐ ܐܳܡܪܺܝܢܰܢ: ܕܢܩܰܒܶܠ ܗܽܘ̈ܠܦܳܢܶܐ ܕܐܰܝܟ ܗܳܢܳܐ ܐܰܘ ܕܢܦܰܫܶܩ ܠܡܫܰܠܡܳܢܽܘܬ݂ܶܗ. ܚܳܣ.
3. ܠܳܐ ܬܓܰܕܶܦ ܕܠܡܳܐ ܠܳܐ ܬܶܬ݂ܚܰܝܰܒ ܒܕܺܝܢܳܐ.
4. ܫܠܺܝܚܶܐ ܐܶܫܬ݁ܰܕܰܪܘ ܕܢܣܰܒܪܽܘܢ ܒܟܽܠ ܕܽܘܟ ܘܒܟܽܠ ܐܰܬ݂ܰܪ.
5. ܐܶܬ݂ܪܰܚܰܡ ܥܰܠ ܐܰܝܟܰܢܳܐ ܕܡܪܰܚܶܡ ܐ̱ܢܳܐ. ܐܳܡܰܪ ܡܳܪܝܳܐ ܡܪܰܚܡܳܢܳܐ.

[2] Properly these are geminate verbs (§25).

Translate into Syriac:

1. The king sent them to the city, and commanded them to speak to the bishop. 2. This is the acceptable (*lit.* accepted) year of the Lord. 3. Take courage (*use the ethpa.*) and speak for (ܣܠܟ) the widow. 4. Let the words of the prophet be expounded unto us. 5. I will not send anyone. There is no one to be sent. 6. Whoever blasphemes against the Holy Spirit shall never be forgiven. 7. I spoke beforehand about all this but at that time you did not accept my words. 8. Honour (*f. pl.*) your father and your mother. 9. Far be it from (*use* ܠ) me to show mercy on a blasphemer. 10. Have mercy (*use the ethpa.*) upon us, o Lord, and send the Holy Spirit to strengthen us.

17. THE APHᶜEL, ETTAPHᶜAL AND OTHER CONJUGATIONS

The aphᶜel generally forms the causative of the verb, as in ܐܩܛܶܠ 'he caused to kill'. The ettaphᶜal is its passive: ܐܶܬܬܰܩܛܰܠ 'he was caused to kill'. *= Hiph Hoph*

Inflection. The whole paradigm of the aphᶜel is as follows. Notice that with preformatives (i.e., in the imperfect, infinitive and participles) the initial ܐ is dropped, and the preformative takes its vowel.

perfect:	sing.	pl.
3rd masc.	ܐܩܛܠ	ܐܩܛܠܘ or ܐܩܛܠܘܢ
3rd fem.	ܐܩܛܠܬ	ܐܩܛܠ (ܐܩܛܠܝ) or ܐܩܛܠܝܢ
2nd masc.	ܐܩܛܠܬ	ܐܩܛܠܬܘܢ
2nd fem.	ܐܩܛܠܬܝ	ܐܩܛܠܬܝܢ
1st	ܐܩܛܠܬ	ܐܩܛܠܢ or ܐܩܛܠܢܢ

imperfect:		
3rd masc.	ܢܩܛܠ	ܢܩܛܠܘܢ
3rd fem.	ܬܩܛܠ (ܢܩܛܠܢ)	ܢܩܛܠܢ
2nd masc.	ܬܩܛܠ	ܬܩܛܠܘܢ
2nd fem.	ܬܩܛܠܝܢ	ܬܩܛܠܢ
1st	ܐܩܛܠ	ܢܩܛܠ

imperative:		
masc.	ܐܩܛܠ	ܐܩܛܠܘ or ܐܩܛܠܘܢ
fem.	ܐܩܛܠܝ	ܐܩܛܠܝ or ܐܩܛܠܝܢ

participles:

active	ܡܰܩܛܶܠ (f. ܡܰܩܛܠܳܐ, f. emph. ܡܰܩܛܠܳܬܳܐ, etc.)
passive	ܡܰܩܛܰܠ (f. ܡܰܩܛܠܳܐ, f. emph. ܡܰܩܛܰܠܬܳܐ, etc.)

infinitive: ܡܰܩܛܳܠܽܘ

If the second radical is a *bgdkpt*, it is pronounced hard everywhere, e.g., ܐܰܟܬܶܒ, ܡܰܟܬܶܒ, etc. As in the paʿel, if the third radical is a guttural or ܪ, the vowel before it is *a*; e.g. ܐܰܥܒܰܪ 'cause to pass'.

A *nomen agentis* in the aphʿel has the form ܡܰܩܛܠܳܢܳܐ. An example is ܝܽܘܚܰܢܳܢ ܡܰܥܡܕܳܢܳܐ 'John the baptizer'.

The paradigm of the ettaphʿal is as follows. (The usual other longer forms exist but are omitted here.)

perfect:

3rd masc.	ܐܶܬܬܰܩܛܰܠ	ܐܶܬܬܰܩܛܰܠܘ
3rd fem.	ܐܶܬܬܰܩܛܠܰܬ	ܐܶܬܬܰܩܛܰܠ
2nd masc.	ܐܶܬܬܰܩܛܰܠܬ	ܐܶܬܬܰܩܛܰܠܬܽܘܢ
2nd fem.	ܐܶܬܬܰܩܛܰܠܬܝ	ܐܶܬܬܰܩܛܰܠܬܶܝܢ
1st	ܐܶܬܬܰܩܛܠܶܬ	ܐܶܬܬܰܩܛܰܠܢ

imperfect:

3rd masc.	ܢܶܬܬܰܩܛܰܠ	ܢܶܬܬܰܩܛܠܽܘܢ
3rd fem.	ܬܶܬܬܰܩܛܰܠ	ܢܶܬܬܰܩܛܠܳܢ
2nd masc.	ܬܶܬܬܰܩܛܰܠ	ܬܶܬܬܰܩܛܠܽܘܢ
2nd fem.	ܬܶܬܬܰܩܛܠܺܝܢ	ܬܶܬܬܰܩܛܠܳܢ
1st	ܐܶܬܬܰܩܛܰܠ	ܢܶܬܬܰܩܛܰܠ

imperative:

masc.	ܐܶܬܬܰܩܛܰܠ	ܐܶܬܬܰܩܛܰܠܘ or ܐܶܬܬܰܩܛܰܠܽܘܢ
fem.	ܐܶܬܬܰܩܛܰܠܝ	ܐܶܬܬܰܩܛܰܠܝ or ܐܶܬܬܰܩܛܰܠܶܝܢ

participle: ܡܶܬܬܰܩܛܰܠ (f. ܡܶܬܬܰܩܛܠܳܐ)

infinitive: ܡܶܬܬܰܩܛܳܠܽܘ

In this paradigm, the sequence -ܐܶܬܬ-, properly -ܐܶܬܬ݂-, is pronounced *eta*, not *etta*; so that ܐܶܬܬܰܩܛܰܠ is *etaqṭal*. Notice that the forms in the impf. beginning with -ܬܬܬ are actually reduced in spelling to -ܬܬ.

Usage and meaning. The causative sense of the aphʿel is the most usual, for example ܥܡܰܕ 'be baptized' – ܐܰܥܡܶܕ 'baptize'. But some verbs in the aphʿel do not fit this description.

a. Sometimes peʿal and aphʿel are more or less the same in meaning, e.g. ܣܒܰܪ and ܐܰܣܒܰܪ 'think, suppose'; ܣܗܶܕ and ܐܰܣܗܶܕ 'testify'.
b. Some verbs have new meanings in the aphʿel, e.g. ܐܰܩܪܶܒ 'fight'. attack
c. Some verbs occur only in the aphʿel, e.g. ܐܰܟܪܶܙ 'preach'.

The anomalous verb ܐܶܫܟܰܚ 'find, be able' may be taken to be an aphʿel of ܫܟܚ in which the vowel of the preformative is *e* instead of *a*. Thus the imperfect is ܢܶܫܟܰܚ and the participle ܡܶܫܟܰܚ and infinitive ܡܶܫܟܳܚܽܘ.

The ettaphʿal is, in fact, somewhat rare. For the passive of the aphʿel, many verbs use the ethpeʿel or ethpaʿal instead, e.g. ܐܶܬܟܪܶܙ 'be preached' (passive of ܐܰܟܪܶܙ).

Other conjugations. A number of verbs of four letters are, etymologically, a three-letter root plus a prefix or infix. For example, ܫܰܥܒܶܕ 'subjugate' derives from the root ܥܒܕ and is accordingly called a shaphʿel. The passive ܐܫܬܚܠܦ is an eshtaphʿal. The shaphʿel/eshtaphʿal conjugation, which is causative in meaning, is the most common of the minor conjugations. Others include the saphʿel (e.g. ܣܲܪܗܒ 'hasten' from ܪܗܒ) and payʿel (ܣܲܝܒܲܪ 'endure' from ܣܒܪ).[1] All these verbs have the *a-e* vowel pattern of the paʿel and are conjugated like other quadriliteral verbs (§16).

Vocabulary

ܟܪܙ	*aph.* preach;	ܫܥܒܕ	*shaph.* subjugate enslave
	ethp. be preached	ܡܠܟ	*aph.* reign
ܥܡܕ	*aph.* baptize	ܠܒܫ	be dressed, *a*;
ܐܫܟܚ	find, be able		*aph.* clothe
ܣܗܕ	*aph.* bear witness	ܡܪܕ	*aph.* fight, attack
ܚܠܦ	*shaph.* change	ܫܠܡ	*aph.* deliver, hand over, commit become a Muslim
ܫܐܕܐ	demon	ܚܘܪ	white
ܐܠܘ	if (contrary to fact)	ܐܝܙܓܕܐ	emissary (Persian word)
ܫܠܝܡܘܢ	Solomon	ܟܢ	then, next
ܟܡܐ	how much, how many	ܠܒܘܫܐ	garment, clothing
ܕܘܝ	wretched, un- happy; *emph.* ܕܘܝܐ	ܒܥܝܪܐ	animal(s) (*f. sing.*)

Exercises

Translate into English:

١. ܘܐܡܠܟ ܫܠܝܡܘܢ ܥܠܐ ܟܠܗ ܐܝܣܪܐܝܠ ܚܠܦ ܐܒܘܗܝ܂

٢. ܠܐ ܬܒܥܐ ܐܝܕܐ ܚܡܪܐ ܡܫܬܚܘܝܢ ܗܘܝܬ ܠܟܡܪ܂

---

[1] For the palpel conjugation, see p. 118 below.

Translate into Syriac:

1. He will preach; we are able; they were attacked. 2. She reigned over the whole nation after her father. 3. I bear witness to you that my word is true and believable (*lit.* believed). 4. Our fathers have handed down (*use* ܡܠܡ) this wisdom to us. 5. John baptized with water, but he will baptize with the Holy Spirit. 6. The wretched (man) was unable to speak. 7. He clothed his teaching (in) the clothing of fine words. 8. Christ is preached, whether (*lit.* if) by us or whether by others. 9. The demons fought against the blessed one, but it was they who were subjugated by him. 10. I know the scriptures, and let him not suppose that they should be changed (*use the eshtaph'al*).

18. OBJECTIVE PRONOMINAL SUFFIXES, I

We have seen that the direct object of a verb may be indicated by the preposition -ܠ with either a noun or a pronoun suffix following. Thus: ܢܩܛܠܲܢ ܠ, 'he will kill us'. There is, however, a more idiomatic way of expressing a pronoun as a direct object, and that is by a suffix on the verb itself. These objective pronominal suffixes are similar to, though not identical with, the possessive suffixes treated in §6. This lesson covers suffixes on the perfect tense of the verb.

The forms of the suffixes are as follows:

	sing.	pl.
1st	ܢܝ	ܢ
2nd m.	ܟ	ܟܘܢ
2nd f.	ܟܝ	ܟܝܢ
3rd m.	ܗܝ, ܝܗܝ, ܝܘܗܝ, ܗܘܝ	—
3rd f.	ܗ	—

There are no suffixes for the 3rd plural, the enclitic forms ܐܢܘܢ and ܐܢܝܢ being used in their place. (Remember that the other personal pronouns are not used as direct objects.)

The forms of the verb to which the suffixes are attached have to be learned separately. For the peʿal pf. these forms are as follows. The vowel that connects verb to suffix is shown separately from the form. For most of the forms it is constant. For others, marked *, it is the same as the vowel in the familiar paradigm of ܩܛܠܬ, ܩܛܠܬܝ, ܩܛܠܬܘܢ, etc., except that the 1st singular suffix is -ܝ.

	sing.	pl.
3rd m.	ܩܛܠܗ-*	ܩܛܠܗ-ܿ
3rd f.	ܩܛܠܗ-*	ܩܛܠ-ܿ
2nd m.	ܩܛܠܟ-ܿ	ܩܛܠܟܘܢ-ܿ
2nd f.	ܩܛܠܟܝ-ܿ	ܩܛܠܟܝܢ-ܿ
1st	ܩܛܠܢ-*	ܩܛܠܢ-ܿ

The entire paradigm for the peʿal perfect is as follows:

singular verb

suffix	3rd m.	3rd f.	2nd m.	2nd f.	1st
no suffix	ܩܛܠ	ܩܛܠܬ	ܩܛܠܬ	ܩܛܠܬܝ	ܩܛܠܬ
1st	ܩܛܠܢܝ	ܩܛܠܬܢܝ	ܩܛܠܬܢܝ	ܩܛܠܬܝܢܝ	—
2nd m.	ܩܛܠܟ	ܩܛܠܬܟ	—	—	ܩܛܠܬܟ
2nd f.	ܩܛܠܟܝ	ܩܛܠܬܟܝ	—	—	ܩܛܠܬܟܝ
3rd m.	ܩܛܠܗ	ܩܛܠܬܗ	ܩܛܠܬܝܗܝ	ܩܛܠܬܝܗܝ	ܩܛܠܬܗ
3rd f	ܩܛܠܗ	ܩܛܠܬܗ	ܩܛܠܬܗ	ܩܛܠܬܝܗ	ܩܛܠܬܗ
1 pl.	ܩܛܠܢ	ܩܛܠܬܢ	ܩܛܠܬܢ	ܩܛܠܬܝܢ	—
2 m. pl.	ܩܛܠܟܘܢ	ܩܛܠܬܟܘܢ	—	—	ܩܛܠܬܟܘܢ
2 f. pl.	ܩܛܠܟܝܢ	ܩܛܠܬܟܝܢ	—	—	ܩܛܠܬܟܝܢ

plural verb

suffix	3rd m.	3rd f.	2nd m.	2nd f.	1st
no suffix	ܩܛܠܘ	ܩܛܠܝ	ܩܛܠܬܘܢ	ܩܛܠܬܝܢ	ܩܛܠܢ
1st	ܩܛܠܘܢܝ	ܩܛܠܝܢܝ	ܩܛܠܬܘܢܢܝ	ܩܛܠܬܝܢܢܝ	—
2nd m.	ܩܛܠܘܟ	ܩܛܠܝܟ	—	—	ܩܛܠܢܟ
2nd f.	ܩܛܠܘܟܝ	ܩܛܠܝܟܝ	—	—	ܩܛܠܢܟܝ
3rd m.	ܩܛܠܘܗܝ	ܩܛܠܝܗܝ	ܩܛܠܬܘܢܝܗܝ	ܩܛܠܬܝܢܝܗܝ	ܩܛܠܢܝܗܝ
3rd f.	ܩܛܠܘܗ	ܩܛܠܝܗ	ܩܛܠܬܘܢܗ	ܩܛܠܬܝܢܗ	ܩܛܠܢܗ
1 pl.	ܩܛܠܘܢ	ܩܛܠܝܢ	ܩܛܠܬܘܢܢ	ܩܛܠܬܝܢܢ	—
2 m. pl.	ܩܛܠܘܟܘܢ	ܩܛܠܝܟܘܢ	—	—	ܩܛܠܢܟܘܢ
2 f. pl.	ܩܛܠܘܟܝܢ	ܩܛܠܝܟܝܢ	—	—	ܩܛܠܢܟܝܢ

Notice in this paradigm:

a. The form of the 3rd m. sing. suffix is determined by the
   vowel connecting it to the verb: after a consonant it is ܗ;
   after ܇ it is ܘܗ (the whole ending is then pronounced *u*),
   after ' it is ܝܗ (*āy*), and after ܇ it is ܝܘ (*iw*).

b. In the 3rd m. and f. sing. (but not the 1st sing.) and 3rd
   f. pl. of the verb, the forms with the ܗܢ and ܗܡ suffixes
   are just the unsuffixed forms with ܗܢ and ܗܡ added.

c. In the 3rd f. pl. and 1st pl. of the verb, which otherwise
   connect to suffixes with ', the 2nd. f. sing. suffix retains
   the vowel ', as in ܫܡܥܢܟܝ, 'we heard you (*f.*)'.

The longer forms of the 3rd m. and f. pl. perfect, ܩܛܠܘܢ
and ܩܛܠܝܢ, can also take suffixes. They have the connecting
vowel '; thus ܩܛܠܘܢܗ, ܩܛܠܘܢܟ, ܩܛܠܝܢܟ, ܩܛܠܝܢܗ, etc.

For verbs with perfect in *e*, the vowel ' becomes ' when on
account of a suffix it moves onto the first syllable; e.g.,
ܣܓܕܗ 'he worshipped it' (but ܣܓܕܬܗ 'she worshipped it').

In the pa'el and aph'el pf., the attachment of suffixes is similar; but in these conjugations the vowel on the second root
letter disappears in the 3rd m. sing. and 3rd m. and f. pl.
before most of the suffixes. Examples of suffixed forms are:

ܐܥܡܕܗ	he baptized her
ܫܕܪܘܗܝ	they (*m.*) sent him
ܩܒܠܘܗܝ	they (*f.*) received him
ܫܪܪܬܢܝ	she strengthened me
ܐܥܡܕܢܝܗܝ	we baptized him.

Pronominal suffixes on verbs cannot be used in a reflexive sense. This sense has to be expressed otherwise, e.g. with ܢܰܦܫܳܐ 'self', as in ܡܰܟܶܟ ܢܰܦܫܶܗ 'he humbled himself'.

A pronoun suffix is often used to anticipate an object already marked by ـܠ, as in ܙܰܒܢܶܗ ܠܟܬܳܒܳܐ 'he bought the book'.

Vocabulary

ܦܣܰܩ	cut, cut off, *o*	ܣܥܰܪ	do, perform,
ܫܰܡܶܫ	*pa.* serve		visit, *o*
ܩܒܰܪ	bury, *o*	ܪܓܶܙ	be angry, *a.*
ܟܪܶܗ	*ethp.* be sick		*aph.* anger
ܟܪܺܝܗ	sick, ill	ܐܶܡܰܬܝ	when?
ܡܣܰܡ ܒܪܺܫܳܐ	punishment	ܟܺܐܢܳܐܝܺܬ	justly
ܒܶܝܬ ܐܰܣܺܝܪ̈ܶܐ	(in) prison	ܝܺܗܘܕܺܝܬ	Judith
ܕܰܘܺܝܕ	David	ܪܗܘܡܳܝܳܐ	Roman (*adj.*)
ܗܓܡܘܢܳܐ	governor	ܓܰܝܳܣܳܐ	robber
ܥܰܪܛܶܠ	naked	ܐܶܦܶܣܳܘܣ	Ephesus
ܣܰܓܝ	(*adv.*) much,	ܓܶܝܪ	for (*conj.; usually*
	greatly		*2nd word in a clause*)
ܐܰܟܣܢܳܝܳܐ	stranger	ـܕ	*introduces direct*
ܡܥܰܪܬܳܐ	cave (*f.*)		*and indirect speech*

Exercises

Translate into English:

١. ܩܡܢ ܘܚܙܰܝܢ ܣܥܰܪ ܘܫܰܡܶܫܟܟܶܗ ܣܗܶܕܟܶܗ.

٢. ܐܰܝܟ ܐܰܚܙܰܝܗܝ ܡܥܰܪܬܳܐ ܘܐܶܡܰܝ ܩܒܰܪܙܶܗ ܠܐܠܗܐܘ.

٣. ܟܣܶܐ ܚܙܳܐ ܠܰܚܙܳܢܳܐ. ܐܢܳܐ ܠܐ ܟܚܙܶܐܗ.

Translate into Syriac, using suffixed forms where possible:

1. Did you (*f. sing.*) receive our letter? We sent it to you.
2. She took the gospel book and expounded it. 3. That is the commandment. Have you (*m. sing.*) heard it? I have heard it and I have kept it. 4. The Romans fought against the Jews and subjugated them under their emperor (*lit.* king). 5. Our emissary was sent to you (*m. pl.*) and you did not receive him. 6. Judith cut off his head, and took it to her companions. 7. If you (*m. pl.*) have killed him, you will not be able to flee from punishment. 8. We have justly angered thee; but thou hast loved us. 9. The emissary was attacked by robbers. They took all that he had and left him. 10. The king was angry toward David because the people were glorifying him.

19. OBJECTIVE PRONOMINAL SUFFIXES, 2

Objective pronominal suffixes may also be attached to the imperfect, imperative, and infinitive of the verb.

Attached to the imperfect. The suffixes are the same as those on the perfect, but the connecting vowels are different.

In the pe'al, those forms of the imperfect without an afformative, i.e., the forms ܢܦܩܘܠ, ܐܦܩܘܠ, ܬܦܩܘܠ, lose the stem vowel (o for most transitive verbs) and attach the suffix with the usual vowels ܢ-, ܝ-, ܗ-, ܟ-; but the 3rd singular suffixes are ܘܗܝ- (m.) and ܗ- (f.). (The suffixes ܗ- and ܗ'- are also found.) With the suffixes ܢܝ- and ܗܝ- the stem vowel reappears and there is no connecting vowel. Those forms with an afformative, that is, ܐܦܩܠܟ, ܬܦܩܠܢ, ܬܦܩܟ, ܐܦܩܠܢ, ܐܦܩܟ, all attach the suffix with the connecting vowel '; except, as in the perfect, the suffix ܗ- retains the vowel '. Examples using the verb ܣܥܪ 'visit' are:

ܢܣܥܕܝܘܗܝ	we shall visit him
ܢܣܥܕܘܟܘܢ	we shall visit you (*m. pl.*)
ܐܣܥܕܘܢܝܗܝ	you (*m. pl.*) will visit him
ܢܣܥܕܢܟܝ	they (*f.*) will visit you (*f. sing.*).

The whole inflection is set out in the paradigm on the next page. This shows all the different endings and suffixes; the forms not shown that begin with -ܐ and -ܐ' can be inferred from it.

	3rd m. s.	2nd f. s.	3rd m. pl.	3rd f. pl.
no suffix	ܢܶܩܛܽܘܠ	ܬܶܩܛܠܺܝܢ	ܢܶܩܛܠܽܘܢ	ܢܶܩܛܠܳܢ
1st	ܢܶܩܛܠܰܢܝ	ܬܶܩܛܠܺܝܢܳܢܝ	ܢܶܩܛܠܽܘܢܳܢܝ	ܢܶܩܛܠܳܢܳܢܝ
2nd m.	ܢܶܩܛܠܳܟ	—	ܢܶܩܛܠܽܘܢܳܟ	ܢܶܩܛܠܳܢܳܟ
2nd f.	ܢܶܩܛܠܶܟܝ	—	ܢܶܩܛܠܽܘܢܶܟܝ	ܢܶܩܛܠܳܢܶܟܝ
3rd m.	ܢܶܩܛܠܺܝܘܗܝ	ܬܶܩܛܠܺܝܢܳܝܗܝ	ܢܶܩܛܠܽܘܢܳܝܗܝ	ܢܶܩܛܠܳܢܳܝܗܝ
	also ܢܶܩܛܠܶܗ			
3rd f.	ܢܶܩܛܠܺܝܗ	ܬܶܩܛܠܺܝܢܳܗ	ܢܶܩܛܠܽܘܢܳܗ	ܢܶܩܛܠܳܢܳܗ
	also ܢܶܩܛܠܳܗ			
1 pl.	ܢܶܩܛܠܰܢ	ܬܶܩܛܠܺܝܢܰܢ	ܢܶܩܛܠܽܘܢܰܢ	ܢܶܩܛܠܳܢܰܢ
2 m. pl.	ܢܶܩܛܘܠܟܽܘܢ	—	ܢܶܩܛܠܽܘܢܟܽܘܢ	ܢܶܩܛܠܳܢܟܽܘܢ
2 f. pl.	ܢܶܩܛܘܠܟܶܝܢ	—	ܢܶܩܛܠܽܘܢܟܶܝܢ	ܢܶܩܛܠܳܢܟܶܝܢ

For the paʿel and the aphʿel the inflection is similar. The vowel on the second root letter vanishes in all the forms except before the suffixes ܟܽܘܢ- and ܟܶܝܢ-. Thus:

ܢܫܰܕܪܺܝܘܗܝ let us send him
ܢܥܰܡܕܟܽܘܢ he will baptize you.

Attached to the imperative. The suffixes give the following forms. Notice the unexpected connecting vowels in the masculine singular. In the plural, suffixes may be attached to both the short and the long forms of the imperative. In both forms of the masculine plural, there is the unexpected vowel ܳ between the first and second root letters.

singular verb

	m.	f.
1st sing.	ܩܛܘܠܝܢܝ	ܩܛܘܠܝܢܝ
3rd m. sing.	ܩܛܘܠܝܗܝ	ܩܛܘܠܝܘܗܝ
3rd f. sing.	ܩܛܘܠܝܗ	ܩܛܘܠܝܗ
1st pl.	ܩܛܘܠܝܢ	ܩܛܘܠܝܢ

plural verb:	short form m.	short form f.	long form m.	long form f.
1st sing.	ܩܛܠܘܢܝ	ܩܛܘܠܝܢܝ	ܩܛܠܘܢܢܝ	ܩܛܘܠܝܢܢܝ
3rd m. sing.	ܩܛܠܘܗܝ	ܩܛܘܠܝܗܝ	ܩܛܠܘܢܝܗܝ	ܩܛܘܠܝܢܝܗܝ
3rd f. sing.	ܩܛܠܘܗ	ܩܛܘܠܝܗ	ܩܛܠܘܢܗ	ܩܛܘܠܝܢܗ
1st pl.	ܩܛܠܘܢ	ܩܛܘܠܝܢ	ܩܛܠܘܢܢ	ܩܛܘܠܝܢܢ

In the paʿel and aphʿel, suffixes are attached to the ordinary forms of the imperative, using the same suffixes and connecting vowels as shown above for the peʿal. In the masculine singular and the masculine long form of the plural, the vowel on the second root letter remains. In other forms it vanishes. Thus:

ܫܰܕܰܪܝܢܝ send (*m.*) me! *but* ܫܰܕܪܝܢܝ send (*f.*) me!
ܩܰܒܠܘܢܝ *or* ܩܰܒܶܠܘܢܢܝ receive (*m.*) me!

The 2nd sing. m. impf. when used with ܠܐ as a prohibition can take the vowel and suffixes of the imperative, as in

ܠܐ ܬܶܩܛܘܠܝܢܝ do not kill me!
ܠܐ ܬܩܰܒܠܝܗܝ do not receive him!

Attached to the infinitive. The infinitive is considered as a noun and the suffixes are the ordinary possessive suffixes (§6) except that the 1st singular suffix is ܢܝ-. Thus from

the infinitive ܩܛܠܐ we have ܩܛܠܟ, ܩܛܠܟܪ, ܩܛܠܟܘܢ,
ܩܛܠܟܝܢ etc. (For this kind of inflection recall §11, p. 50
above.) In the pa'el and aph'el, the infinitives add a ܬ before
taking the suffixes, and so become feminine nouns like
ܡܠܟܘܬܐ. Thus from the infinitive ܡܩܛܠܘ we have
ܡܩܛܠܘܬܟ, ܡܩܛܠܘܬܝ, ܡܩܛܠܘܬܗ, etc. Note that the suffixes are still objective: ܩܛܠܟ means 'to kill me' and not
'for me to kill (someone else)'.

Vocabulary

ܙܒܢ	*pa.* sell	ܕܒܚ	*pe., pa.* sacrifice
ܦܠܚ	work, till, serve, *o*	ܡܠܐܟܐ	angel
ܕܐܡܪ	*particle indicating*	ܒܒܠ	Babylon
	direct speech	ܥܠܬܐ	reason, cause,
ܩܫܝܫ	old		explanation (*f.*)
ܚܩܠܐ	field (*f.*)	ܬܓܪܐ	merchant
ܐܘܢܬܐ	opinion, mind (*f.*)	ܘܡܪܢܐ	monk
ܦܘܛܝܦܪ	Potiphar	ܛܝܡܐ	(*pl.*) price

Exercises

Translate into English:

١. ܡܕܝܢ: ܠܐ ܐܘܣܦܘ ܠܡܐܟܠܗ. ܡܚܕܦܝܘܗܝ ܗ/ܦܠܣܛܝܘܗܝ.

٢. ܐܢ ܐܚܪܘܒܝܗ ܠܡܕܝܢܬܗ ܠܐ ܢܚܕܬܘܢܗ ܐܚܬܗܐܬܗ.

٣. ܐܡܠܟ ܦܪܥܘܢ ܥܠܝܗܘܢ ܗܘܘ ܘܢܥܒܕܗܡ ܡܕܝܢܐ.

٤. ܐܢ ܐܢܐ ܠܟܪ ܘܚܣܡܐ ܠܡܬܕܒܚܘ: ܠܐ ܐܩܢܬܟܗ ܟܡ ܘܐܝܟܐ ܐܢܐ
ܚܣܝܪ ܘܠܚܩܘܪ.

٥. ܚܘܟܕܐ ܗܢܐ ܢܩܫܝܫܐ ܘܣܒܗ ܘܘܡܢܐ ܗܠܐ ܗܟܠܝ ܠܒܝܬܢܐ ܠܡܬܕܟܠܘܬܗ.

6. ܐܢܐ: ܗܘܐ ܡܦܠܚܒ. ܗܠ ܡܠܠܐܠܐ ܗܢ ܚܡܟܡܐ ܢܚܙܐ ܟܠܪ ܡܪܡܪ
ܘܢܠܚܙ ܡܢܗ ܠܠ ܐܡܚܟܠܘܘܢ.

7. ܚܢܬ ܥܕܡܦܕ ܐܚܕܘܘܢ ܠܐܣܦܘܘܢ ܠܠܡܝܪܙܐ. ܘܗܝ ܐܚܠܗ ܗܦܠܡܦܒ:
ܡܠܘܘܢ.

8. ܡܢܗܠܐ ܘܐܢܦܡܝ ܐܘܕܢܝ ܗܢܠܐ ܗܘܐ ܠܟܡ ܢܠܟܠܐ ܘܗܕܡܪܠܐ ܗܢܐ: ܚܕܘܘܙܢܠܐ
ܘܐܠܚܗܐ ܠܩܟܠܠܐ ܡܩܟܠܠܐ ܠܩܠܢܐ ܘܠܩܡܩܡܝܢܐ.

9. ܗܩܡ ܒܙܢܠܐ ܘܠܢܥܥܠܚܐܠܢܝܘܢ ܠܠܝܚܢܐ ܗܢ ܗܪܡܚܘܘܢ. ܘܗܚܕܐܘܘܢ ܠܟܡ
ܠܠܠܥܥܗܠܐ ܗܢܐ ܚܡܗ ܐܡܩܢܐ.

10. ܗܝܢܙܠܐ ܘܗܡܥܚܕܗ ܗܢ ܐܠܚܡܢܬܪܘܘܢ ܐܘܕܢܝ ܘܘܗܗ: ܢܡܡܡܐ ܗܘܐ ܡܠܠܚܠܐ
ܗܘܙܐ. ܡܠܢܗ ܡܥܡܡܩܣ ܠܠܡܡܡܝܕܢܗ.

Translate into Syriac:

1. The Lord is God; let us worship him and glorify him.
2. This is the son; let us kill him.   3. I have handed you (*m.
pl.*) over to the king of Babylon, you and the whole people,
that you should serve him.   4. Let them buy the fruit and
taste it.   5. He knows my opinion, and he cannot change it.
6. I shall be betrayed (handed over) into the hands of the
Romans, and they shall kill me.   7. She had a field, and her
brother used to say to her, 'Sell it for (-ܟ) a good price.'
8. My daughters, fear not. They will not find you and they
will not kill you.   9. The governor commanded his servants,
'Take her to prison.'   10. This teaching is blasphemy and I
cannot accept it.

20. WEAK VERBS. PE-NUN VERBS

Weak verbs. Variations in the conjugation of verbs are generally produced by the presence in the stem of (*a*) a *nun* as a first radical, (*b*) one of the letters *alaph*, *waw*, *yod*, or (*c*) a doubled or repeated second radical. The resulting classes, with examples, are:

1.	*pe-nun*	نفَم
2.	*pe-alaph*	أَكَلا
3.	*pe-yod*	نَهُد
4.	*'e-alaph*	هُلاا
5.	hollow (or *'e-waw*)	(مومر) هُمد
6.	geminate (or double *'e*)	(حال) كَا
7.	*lamad-yod*	سبُنا , حخُا

Verbs with a guttural letter or ; as the third radical, like حمكَلا and حَبَر, are sometimes considered as another class of weak verbs, but their peculiarities are slight and we have already treated them along with the strong verb.

It is possible for a verb to be doubly weak (e.g., أَلَا 'come'), though certain peculiarities are never found together. For example if a verb beginning with a *nun* has a vowel letter as its second radical (e.g., نوحا 'rest'), it is not weak in the same way as the *pe-nun* verbs.

Pe-nun verbs. As will have been already noticed in such words as أَنَا and محَبَلا the letter *nun* shows a tendency to become assimilated to a following consonant when no vowel-sound intervenes between the two. (The effect of this assimilation is to double the following letter, as shown by the *qushaya* on ܬ in ܐܰܢ̱ܬ݁ for example.) In *pe-nun* verbs, the assimilation takes place in the peʿal imperfect and infinitive and throughout the aphʿel and ettaphʿal. In these forms the assimilated *nun* is not written at all. Additionally, in the peʿal imperative, the *nun* disappears altogether.

The following paradigm gives the affected forms of ܢܦܰܩ ('go out') in the peʿal:

imperfect	sing.	pl.
3rd m.	ܢܶܦܽܘܩ	ܢܶܦܩܽܘܢ
3rd f.	ܬܶܦܽܘܩ (ܬܶܦܽܘܩ)	ܢܶܦܩܳܢ
2nd m.	ܬܶܦܽܘܩ	ܬܶܦܩܽܘܢ
2nd f.	ܬܶܦܩܺܝܢ	ܬܶܦܩܳܢ
1st	ܐܶܦܽܘܩ	ܢܶܦܽܘܩ

imperative	sing.	pl.
m.	ܦܽܘܩ	ܦܽܘܩܽܘ, ܦܽܘܩܽܘܢ
f.	ܦܽܘܩܝ	ܦܽܘܩܝ, ܦܽܘܩܶܝܢ

infinitive: ܡܶܦܰܩ

In the aphʿel ('put out, expel'), we have:

perfect ܐܰܦܶܩ, ܐܰܦܩܰܬ, ܐܰܦܩܶܬ, ܐܰܦܶܩܬܝ, ܐܰܦܶܩܘ, ܐܰܦܶܩܬܽܘܢ, etc.

imperfect ܢܰܦܶܩ, ܬܰܦܶܩ, ܬܰܦܩܺܝܢ, ܐܰܦܶܩ, ܢܰܦܩܽܘܢ, ܬܰܦܩܳܢ, ܢܰܦܶܩ, etc.

imperative ܐܰܦܶܩ, ܐܰܦܶܩܝ, ܐܰܦܶܩܘ, ܐܰܦܶܩܶܝܢ

participles: active ܡܰܦܶܩ, passive ܡܰܦܰܩ

infinitive ܡܰܦܳܩܽܘ

The ettaphʿal is ܐܶܬܬܰܦܰܩ, etc.

The verb ܢܬܠ ('give') is used only in the peʿal imperfect, where it takes the vowel *e* (ܢܶܬܶܠ, ܬܶܬܶܠ, ܬܶܬܠܽܘܢ, etc.), and in the infinitive (ܡܶܬܰܠ). For other forms, a different verb, ܝܗܒ (§22) is used.

The verb ܣܠܶܩ ('go up') is irregular in that it assimilates the *lamad* just as a *pe-nun* verb assimilates the *nun*. Thus in the affected forms it is conjugated in the same way: impf. ܢܶܣܰܩ, inf. ܡܶܣܰܩ; aphʿel ('bring up, send up') pf. ܐܰܣܶܩ, impf. ܢܰܣܶܩ, inf. ܡܰܣܳܩܽܘ, participle act. ܡܰܣܶܩ, pass. ܡܰܣܰܩ.

Vocabulary

ܢܦܰܩ	go out, *o*; *aph*. expel	ܢܶܬܶܠ	(*impf*.) give
ܢܚܶܬ	go down, *o*	ܢܦܰܠ	fall, *e*
ܢܣܰܟ	pour, *o*	ܢܛܰܪ	keep, *a*
ܢܣܰܒ	take, *a*	ܣܠܶܩ	go up; *impf*. ܢܶܣܰܩ
ܢܓܰܕ	draw, *e*	ܢܩܶܦ	adhere, cling , *a*
ܡܽܘܠܟܳܢܳܐ	promise	ܡܶܫܚܳܐ	oil
ܐܶܓܳܪܳܐ	roof	ܡܫܰܚ	anoint, *o*
ܐܰܗܪܽܘܢ	Aaron	ܦܳܪܽܘܩܳܐ	saviour
ܚܰܝܶܐ	(*pl*.) life, salvation		

Exercises

Translate into English:

1. ܒܗܰܘ ܝܰܘܡܳܐ ܗܰܘ ܕܥܰܠ ܐܶܓܳܪܳܐ ܠܳܐ ܢܶܚܽܘܬ ܠܡܶܣܰܒ ܡܶܕܶܡ ܕܒܰܝܬܶܗ.
2. ܡܶܛܽܠ ܐܳܘܟܳܐ ܗܽܘܳܐ ܚܶܕܽܘ ܐܺܝܬܰܘܗ̱ܝ ܡܽܘܠܟܳܢܳܐ ܕܰܐܠܳܗܳܐ ܕܶܐܬܶܠܺܝܘܗܝ ܠܗ
ܠܟܽܘܢ ܘܠܰܒܢܰܝܟܽܘܢ.
3. ܦܠܳܢ ܕܦܩܶܕ ܠܗܽܘܳܐ ܗܳܢܳܐ ܕܶܐܬܥܰܠܰܠ ܘܢܶܦܶܠ ܒܢܽܘܪܳܐ: ܐܶܬܶܠ ܠܗ.

4. ܠ܂ ܐܩܚ ܡܢ ܐܘܠܐ ܐܝܢ ܩܠܐ ܠܝܢ ܠܚܠܐܢ܂

5. ܘܡܩܟܡ ܢܡܘܢ ܠܩܚܡܠܐ ܘܐܩܚ ܠܐܡܟܝ ܘܐܚܢܝ ܘܡܕܐܚܢܝ ܝܘܗ ܐܡܝ܂

6. ܚܢܒ ܡܩ ܠܫܡܥܩܠ ܘܠܐ ܐܚܚܘܩܡܘ ܘܐܠܗܘ ܩܠܘܗܢ ܥܩܣܢ܂

7. ܐܩܩܒܘ ܐܢܝ܊ܐ ܘܐܩܩ ܠܒܘܐ ܘܘܐܠܐܝܚ ܠܝܝ܊ܐܐ ܠܐܩܣܡܘܢܩܠ܂

8. ܩܠܘܐ ܐܡܐܚܟܒܘ ܠܡܩܟܢܫܐ ܘܐܩܚܡ ܗܝ܊ܢܐܐ ܚܡܩܚܘ ܘܡܢܘܗܢ܂

9. ܩܚ ܢܡܢܠ ܘܡܘܡܝ ܚܢܩܗܘ ܘܐܘܘܢ ܘܡܩܘܫܚܘܢ܂

10. ܐܝܚ ܝܘܐ ܠܟܘ ܠܩܠܚܠ ܡܩܠܩܠ ܡܢ ܩܢܘܗܠ ܘܐܗܝ܊ܘ ܠܟܢ ܥܡ ܡܝ ܐܠܩܩܢܒ ܝܘܘܘ ܢܩܠܐ ܠܟܡ ܘܠܩܩܠܚܩܐܡ ܩܠܚܠ ܘܥܢܠ܂

Letter to Abgar

Translate into Syriac:

1. Be careful lest you fall.   2. It is fearsome to fall into the hands of God.   3. Bring out the oil and pour it.   4. Come down from the roof and go out into the field.   5. If you (*pl.*) love me, keep my commandments.   6. It is not fitting to go up to the temple without a sacrifice to offer.   7. Do not expel (*use* ܢܦܩ) me from the church.   8. The priest said to the women, I shall receive whatever you give me.   9. I am speaking to those of you who suppose that you can keep the whole law.   10. If we can give good (things) to our children, then (*use* ܘܝ) will not God give us the Holy Spirit?

98

21. PE-ALAPH VERBS

This class includes some very common verbs such as ܐܟܰܠ
'eat', ܐܶܡܰܪ 'say', and ܐܶܙܰܠ 'go'. The peculiarities of *pe-alaph*
verbs can be considered under four headings, of which the
first two are general rules, already familiar (§3), involving
alaph.

1. *Alaph* must have a vowel at the beginning of a word or
syllable. (This is the same rule that dictated the form
ܐܶܗܡܶܐ for the 1st sing. pa'el impf.) For the pe'al of *pe-
alaph* verbs this rule affects some forms of the perfect, the
passive participle, and the imperative. In the perfect the
vowel to be supplied is *e*, as in ܐܶܟܰܠ (not ܐܟܰܠ), 'he ate'. In
the passive participle the vowel is *a*, as in ܐܰܚܪܶܒ 'destroyed'.
In the imperative, it is usually also *a*, e.g. ܐܰܟܽܘܠ 'eat!'; but it
is *e* for those verbs whose stem vowel in the imperfect is *a*,
e.g. ܐܶܡܰܪ 'say!'. This rule also affects the perfect and imperfect ethpe'el: the vowel on *alaph* is *e*, as in ܐܶܬܐܣܰܪ (or rather,
ܐܶܬܐܰܣܰܪ: see the next rule), 'he was bound'.

2. *Alaph* gives up its vowel to a preceding consonant that
has no vowel. (This rule is familiar from words with an
inseparable prefix, e.g. ܘܰܐܒܐ 'of the father', §4.) Thus we
have ܐܶܬܐܰܣܰܪ for ܐܶܬܐܣܰܪ as just mentioned. It also affects the
pa'el imperfect generally: e.g. ܢܰܠܶܟ (not ܢܐܰܠܶܟ) 'he will
compel'.

Besides these two general rules, there are two more specific
peculiarities of *pe-alaph* verbs.

3. In the peʿal imperfect, the vowel of the preformative is *e*
when the stem vowel is *o*, e.g. نُاسفو 'he will hold'. (In other
words, for these verbs the impf. is regular just like نمجفﻻ.)
But when the stem vowel is *a*, the vowel of the preformative
is *i*, as in نُاهَذ 'he will say'. There are only a few *pe-alaph*
verbs with imperfects in *a*, but they include the common
ones ﻻاآ, اهَذ, and اكَذ. For these verbs, the peʿal infinitive
has the same vowel *i* on the preformative, e.g. مُﻻاهَذ 'to say'.

4. In the aphʿel, after the preformatives هَذ- اَذ- نَذ- تَذ- *alaph*
changes to *waw*, giving مَهَو- اَهو- نَهو- تَهو-.[1] The same *waw* appears in the ettaphʿal, shaphʿel and eshtaphʿal. Thus from
اكَذ 'perish' the aphʿel is زوهَذ 'destroy, lose' and ettaphʿal
تَﻻاهوكَذ. The root اسم is only found in the aphʿel زوهسَذ and
eshtaphʿal زوهَهَكهَذ, both meaning 'delay'.

In all these verbs the 1st sing. imperfect is written with only
one *alaph*, e.g. اُهَذ (not اُهَذاذ) 'I will say'.

The following paradigm summarizes the peculiarities of
these verbs.

Peʿal perfect اكَذ, اهَذ, تَهَكَذ, تَهكَذ, اهكَذ, حكَذ, ﻰمكَهَكَذ, etc.
       imperfect in *o* ﻻاهفذ, اكحﻻاَذ, اكحهَذﻻاَذ, اهفﻻاَذ, اهفﻻ, etc.
       imperfect in *a* تَهَذ, نَهﻻاَذ, اسنهﻻاَذ, تَهﻻاَذ, etc.
       imperative in *o* ﻻاهفجِذ ; in *a* تَهَذ
       participle active اُفﻻ ; passive ﻻاُفﻻ
       infinitive for verbs in *o* ﻻاكَذاهُذ ; for verbs in *a* تَهَذاهُذ.

---

[1] In one verb, اَﻻ 'come', the aphʿel has تَ- instead of تَهو-; thus,
تَهسَذ 'bring'. This verb is treated with verbs *lamad-yod* (§27).

Ethpeʿel perfect ܐܬܐܟܠ, ܐܬܐܟܠܬ, ܐܬܐܟܠܬ, ܐܬܐܟܠܬ, etc.
imperfect ܢܬܐܟܠ, ܬܬܐܟܠܘܢ, ܢܬܐܟܠܘܢ, etc.
imperative m. sing. ܐܬܐܟܠ or ܐܬܐܟܠ
participle m. ܡܬܐܟܠ, f. ܡܬܐܟܠܐ
infinitive ܡܬܐܟܠܘ.

Paʿel imperfect ܢܐܟܪ, ܐܟܪ (1st. sing.), ܢܐܟܪܘܢ, etc.
participle active m. ܡܐܟܪ, f. ܡܐܟܪܐ; passive ܡܐܟܪ
infinitive ܡܐܟܪܘ.

Ethpaʿal pf. ܐܬܐܟܪ etc.; impf. ܢܬܐܟܪ etc.; inf. ܡܬܐܟܪܘ.

Aphʿel pf. ܐܘܒܕ, ܐܘܒܕܬ, etc.; impf. ܢܘܒܕ, etc.; inf. ܡܘܒܕܘ.

Ettaphʿal pf. ܐܬܬܘܒܕ etc.; impf. ܢܬܬܘܒܕ etc.; inf. ܡܬܬܘܒܕܘ.

The verb ܐܠܦ 'teach' is conjugated like a paʿel verb in this class, except that after a preformative the *alaph* is not usually written; e.g., ܬܠܦ (rather than ܬܐܠܦ) 'she will teach', and ܡܠܦ 'teaching' (compare ܡܠܦܢܐ 'teacher').[2]

The verb ܐܚܕ 'hold' has an irregular ethpeʿel, in which the ܐ changes to ܬ; thus, ܐܬܬܚܕ (*etḥeḏ*) 'was held' or 'was closed'.

In the verb ܐܙܠ 'go', some forms have an elided pronunciation in which the -ܠ- is silent and its vowel moves back to the ܙ. This happens in such forms as ܐܙܠܬ (*ezaṯ*; not ܐܙܠܬ) 'she went' and ܐܙܠܐ (*āzā*) 'going' (*f.*). This verb also has the irregular imperative ܙܠ 'go!'.

[2] But in dictionaries this verb is usually found under the root ܝܠܦ 'learn', and treated as an irregular aphʿel or paʿel.

Passive participles can sometimes be active in meaning. This is the case with the verb ܐܒܠ/; thus ܗܘܘ ܐܒܝܠܝܢ 'they were mourning'. The passive participle of the verb ܐܚܕ/ can have the expected meaning, as in ܐܚܝܕ ܒܫܢܬܐ 'held in sleep – fast asleep'; but more usually it is active, as in ܐܚܝܕ ܫܪܪܐ 'holding to the truth' and ܐܚܝܕ ܟܠ 'holding all – omnipotent' (a common epithet of God).

Vocabulary

ܐܙܠ/	go, a	ܐܘܚܪ/	aph. delay
ܐܚܕ/	hold, seize (+ܒ), close, o	ܐܡܪ/	say, a
		ܐܠܦ/	teach
ܐܠܨ/	pe.(o), pa. press, compel, oppress	ܐܒܠ/	pass. ptc. ܐܒܝܠ mourning; ethp. mourn
ܐܟܠ/	eat, consume, o		
ܐܒܕ/	perish, be lost, a; aph. destroy, lose	ܐܫܕ/	pour out, shed, o
		ܐܣܪ/	bind, o
ܦܬܚ	open, a	ܬܪܥܐ/	gate, door
ܐܡܬܝ -ܘ	when	ܩܘܫܬܐ	truth (m.)
ܚܕܬܐ	new; emph. ܚܕܬܐ, f. emph. ܚܕܬܐ	ܩܘܪܒܢܐ	offering, eucharist
		ܦܠܚܐ	soldier
ܕܡܥܬܐ/	tear (of the eye; f.); pl. ܕܡܥܐ	ܢܘܪܐ/	fire (f.)
		ܚܝ	living

Exercises

Translate into English:

١. ܡܢ ܘܠܐܚܦܘ ܟܪܡܗܐ ܘܐܢܬܗ: ܚܐܝܢܬܐ ܢܬܐܚܘܢ ܘܬܕܗ.

٢. ܐܡܪ ܗܘܐ ܬܠܡܝܕܐ: ܐܠܐ ܐܡܪ ܠܐܡܗܘ ܘܡܬܐ ܟܕܐܒܐܗ.

Translate into Syriac:

1. Do not say, 'What shall we eat?' 2. I have found the book that was lost. 3. Let us hold to (*use* -ܒ) that which we have received, lest we fall. 4. She said to him, 'Eat!' But he was not able to eat anything. 5. She came out and the door closed after her. 6. Pour out the blood from the offering before you offer it. 7. Christ was handed over to death, but death could not hold him. 8. Go, flee, and do not delay; for he who delays will perish. 9. They were going to seize the saint and bind him and lead him before the governor. 10. The governor commanded him, 'Say what this new doctrine is that you are teaching.'

22. PE-YOD VERBS

This (not very large) class of verbs is sometimes called *pe-yod* and *waw*. A *waw* does appear in the aph'el and ettaph'al of most of them, but in the pe'al, all the verbs in this class begin with *yod*.[1]

The first peculiarity of these verbs arises from the rule for *yod* already met in §3. When a *yod* would not have a full vowel, it assumes the vowel *i*. This happens in some forms of the pe'al perfect and imperative, and throughout the ethpe'el; thus, ܝܺܪܶܬ (not ܝܪܶܬ) 'he inherited'. As a matter of spelling, *alaph* is sometimes prefixed to ـܝ at the beginning of a word, e.g. ܐܺܝܪܶܬ (= ܝܺܪܶܬ). If there is a consonant before the *yod*, the vowel *i* is pronounced with it, as in ܐܶܬܝܺܠܶܕ *etiled* 'was born'; ܕܝܺܪܶܬ *diret* 'who inherited'.

In those forms in which the *yod* is a consonant with a vowel already, the conjugation is regular, e.g. ܝܶܪܬܶܬ 'I inherited', ܐܶܬܝܰܠܕܰܬ 'she was born'. This is the case throughout the pa'el and ethpa'al, e.g. ܝܰܒܶܠ 'transmit', ܐܶܬܝܰܒܰܠ 'be transmitted'.

The vowel of the pe'al perfect is *e* for all *pe-yod* verbs except those that end in a guttural or ܪ, e.g. ܝܺܩܰܪ 'be heavy'. The vowel of the imperfect is always *a*.

In the imperfect and infinitive pe'al, the first root letter *yod* is replaced by *alaph*, and the vowel on this syllable is *i*.

---

[1] The only verb forms in Syriac that actually begin with *waw* are ܘܳܠܶܐ 'be fitting' (§14) and ܘܰܥܶܕ 'appoint'.

Thus we have ܢܺܐܪܰܬ 'he will inherit' and ܡܺܐܪܰܬ 'to inherit'; also ܐܺܪܰܬ 'I shall inherit'. This is a borrowing from the *pe-alaph* verbs and imitates verbs like ܐܶܡܰܪ.

In the aphʿel and ettaphʿal, most *pe-yod* verbs change the *yod* to *waw*. Thus we have ܐܰܘܠܶܕ 'cause to bear – beget'. Two verbs, ܝܺܢܶܩ 'suck (milk)' and ܝܠܠ (which occurs in the aphʿel only), retain the *yod*: ܐܰܝܢܶܩ 'suckle' and ܐܰܝܠܶܠ 'wail'.

The following forms will serve as a guide to conjugation:

peʿal	perfect	ܝܺܪܶܬ (ܐܺܝܪܶܬ)	
	imperfect	ܢܺܐܪܰܬ	
	imperative	ܝܺܪܰܬ (ܐܺܝܪܰܬ)	
	infinitive	ܡܺܐܪܰܬ	
	participles	act. ܝܳܪܶܬ	pass. ܝܪܺܝܬ (ܐܺܝܪܺܝܬ)
ethpeʿel		ܐܶܬܺܝܪܶܬ	
paʿel and ethpaʿal		ܝܰܒܶܠ, ܐܶܬܝܰܒܰܠ	
aphʿel		ܐܰܘܪܶܬ	ܐܰܝܢܶܩ
ettaphʿal		ܐܶܬܬܰܘܪܰܬ	ܐܶܬܬܰܝܢܰܩ

The two verbs ܝܺܬܶܒ 'sit' and ܝܺܕܰܥ 'know' are irregular. In the peʿal imperfect, imperative and infinitive they lose the *yod* and are conjugated like *pe-nun* verbs. ܝܬܒ is further irregular in having its impf. in *e*. Thus for these verbs we have:

peʿal	perfect	ܝܺܬܶܒ	ܝܺܕܰܥ
	imperfect	ܢܺܬܶܒ	ܢܶܕܰܥ
	imperative	ܬܶܒ	ܕܰܥ
	infinitive	ܡܶܬܰܒ	ܡܶܕܰܥ
	participles	ܝܳܬܶܒ, ܝܬܺܝܒ	ܝܳܕܰܥ, ܝܕܺܝܥ

The verb ܝܗܒ 'give' appears only in the perfect, imperative, and participles. (For the imperfect and infinitve, recall that the verb ܢܬܠ is used instead.) The imperative is irregular: ܗܒ. In the peʿal pf. the ܗ is written with *linea occultans* and not pronounced in the following forms: ܝܗܒ, ܝܗܒܬ, ܝܗܒܬܝ, ܝܗܒܘ, ܝܗܒܬܘܢ, ܝܗܒܬܝܢ, ܝܗܒܢ; that is, all except ܝܗܒܬ and ܝܗܒܬ. This irregularity does not extend to the ethpeʿel, which is ܐܬܝܗܒ etc. as usual for a *pe-yod* verb.

Vocabulary

ܝܬܪ	gain, abound, remain over	ܝܕܥ	know; *aph*. inform, make known
ܝܩܕ	burn (*intransitive*); *aph*. *transitive*	ܝܒܠ	*aph*. bring, carry; *pa*. transmit
ܝܨܦ	be anxious, take care	ܝܫܛ	*aph*. stretch out
ܝܠܕ	give birth to; *ethp*. be born; *aph*. beget	ܝܪܬ	inherit
ܝܬܒ	sit, dwell	ܝܗܒ	give
ܟܐܢܘܬܐ	justice, righteousness	ܝܠܦ	learn
ܝܡܝܢܐ	right, right hand (*f*.)	ܐܠܐ	unless
ܟܪܣܐ	womb (*f*.)	ܣܡܠܐ	left, left hand (*f*.)
ܚܘܒܐ	love	ܦܓܪܐ	body
ܝܬܝܪ	more (+ܡܢ than)	ܓܢܬܐ	garden (*f*.)
ܗܪܘܕܣ	Herod	ܦܪ̈ܝܫܐ	Pharisees

Exercises

Translate into English:

1. ܛܥܝܢܐ ܗܘܐ ܐܬܝܒܠܬ ܠܗ ܡܢ ܐܒܘܗܝ.

Translate into Syriac:

1. The woman gave the fruit to the man.   2. Take (*pl.*) the food that remains over, so that nothing may be lost (perish). 3. The priest stretches out his hand over the offering and says this prayer.   4. Give (*pl.*) praise to God, who has caused us to inherit eternal life.   5. The Lord said to my lord, Sit at my right hand.   6. They found the book and brought it to the bishop.   7. Does the promise belong to others? No, we have inherited it.   9. You should know that some deeds are more honourable than others.   8. Adam begot other sons and daughters, who were born outside the garden.   10. In those days they will not say 'Know the Lord' because they shall all know me.

23. ʿE-ALAPH VERBS

The same rules about *alaph* that affected the *pe-alaph* verbs (§21) also affect these verbs. An *alaph* without a full vowel either acquires one, or if it comes after a vowel, it becomes quiescent. An *alaph* with a vowel gives it up to a preceding vowelless consonant and likewise becomes quiescent.

In the peʿal perfect all the verbs in this class have the vowel *e*. For the verb ܫܐܠ 'ask', the 3rd m. sing. is therefore ܫܐܶܠ (from ܫܐܠ). The quiescent *alaph* makes all the other forms of the peʿal perfect start the same way, with ܫܐܠ-; thus: ܫܐܠܟ, ܫܐܠܬܝ, ܫܐܠܬ, ܫܐܠܬ, etc.

In the imperfect peʿal, the vowel is always *a*, but in those parts with an afformative the *alaph* (or rather, the preceding consonant) takes the vowel *e*. The imperfect is thus:

	sing.	pl.
3rd masc.	ܢܫܐܠ	ܢܫܐܠܘܢ
3rd fem.	ܬܫܐܠ	ܢܫܐܠܢ
2nd masc.	ܬܫܐܠ	ܬܫܐܠܘܢ
2nd fem.	ܬܫܐܠܝܢ	ܬܫܐܠܢ
1st	ܐܫܐܠ	ܢܫܐܠ

The other forms of the peʿal follow from the same rules for the quiescence of *alaph*:

imperative	ܫܐܠ
infinitive	ܡܫܐܠ
active participle	m. ܫܐܶܠ f. ܫܐܠܐ
passive participle	ܫܐܝܠ

The ethpeʿel perfect is ܐܫܬܐܠ etc., except that the usual forms of the 3rd fem. sing. and 1st sing. are ܐܫܬܐܠܬ and ܐܫܬܐܠܬ (not ܐܫܬܐܠܬ and ܐܫܬܐܠܬ as expected). In the ethpeʿel imperfect, as in the peʿal, the vowel *e* appears in forms with an afformative, e.g. ܢܫܬܐܠܘܢ.

The paʿel and ethpaʿal are regular: ܫܐܠ, ܐܫܬܐܠ.

The aphʿel is ܐܫܐܠ, ܐܫܐܠܬ (notice the *e*), etc. In the fem. active participle the vowel *e* is likewise found: ܡܫܐܠܐ (for ܡܫܐܠܐ). The aphʿel passive participle is not used.

The verb ܒܐܫ 'be bad' is used impersonally in the peʿal, as in

ܒܬܪ ܐܠܗܐ ܐܚܪܢܐ ܠܐ ܬܐܙܠܘܢ ܕܢܒܐܫ ܠܟܘܢ	Do not go after other gods to your own hurt (*lit.* so that it would be bad for you).

The ethpeʿel ܐܬܒܐܫ (also an alternative form ܐܬܒܐܫ) 'be displeasing' likewise has this impersonal use, as in

ܐܬܒܐܫ ܠܩܐܝܢ ܛܒ	Cain was very displeased.

The aphʿel ܐܒܐܫ is 'do evil'.

The form ܥܬܝܕ. This, the passive particple of ܥܬܕ 'prepare', is used before an infinitive or imperfect with the sense of 'is going to'; e.g.

ܡܢܐ ܥܬܝܕܢ ܠܡܥܒܕ	what are they (*f.*) going to do?
ܟܠ ܐܬܪ ܕܥܬܝܕ ܗܘܐ ܠܡܐܙܠ	every place he was going to go
ܥܬܝܕܐ ܕܬܬܗܦܟ ܠܒܝܬܗ	she is going to return home.

Vocabulary

ܫܐܠ	ask; *pa.* interrogate; *ethp.* decline (+ ܡܢ) ܫܐܠ (ܒ)ܫܠܡܐ greet	ܡܐܢ	be wearisome
ܢܫܩ	*pe.* (*o*, *a*), *pa.* kiss	ܣܐܒ	grow old, be old
ܛܐܒ	be good; *aph.* do good	ܒܐܫ	be bad; *aph.* do evil
ܚܪܝܢܐ	dispute, contention	ܣܥܪ	*ethpa.* be done, take place
ܐܝܩܪܐ	honour	ܗܦܟ	return, go back, *o*
ܕܠܡܐ	perhaps (*in rhetorical questions*)	ܥܝܢܐ	eye (*f.*)
		ܡܘܗܒܬܐ	gift (*f.*)
		ܙܥܘܪܐ	small; *f.* ܙܥܘܪܬܐ
		ܛܒ	very (much)

Exercises

Translate into English:

1. ܠܐ ܡܫܟܚ ܐܢܐ ܕܐܫܐܠ ܠܟܘܢ ܕܗܘܬ ܒܫܐܠܬܟܘܢ.
2. ܠܐ ܐܒܐܫ ܒܚܢܢܝܢ ܕܫܐܠܬ ܡܢܢ ܡܘܗܒܬܐ.
3. ܘܐܡܪ ܡܪܢܐ ܠܬܠܡܝܕܘܗܝ: ܗܦܘܟܘ ܠܐܘܪܚܐ ܕܐܬܝܬܘܢ ܘܐܛܐܒ ܠܟܘܢ.
4. ܗܦܟ ܛܠܝܐ ܠܚܩܠܐ ܘܠܡܕܝܢܬܗ ܟܕ ܡܫܬܐܠ ܡܢ ܐܝܩܪܐ ܕܚܪܝܢܐ.
5. ܘܡܫܐܠܝܢ ܗܘܘ ܠܗ ܡܛܠ ܡܫܝܚܘܬܗ ܘܡܛܠ ܡܠܦܢܘܬܗ. ܗܘ ܕܝܢ ܡܫܬܐܠ ܗܘܐ ܡܢ ܕܠܡܐܡܪ ܡܕܡ.
6. ܠܐ ܐܬܐܠܝܬܘܢ ܒܗܘ ܐܠܦܐ ܐܚܪܢܐ: ܠܡܫܡܥ ܐܦ ܘܠܡܫܡܫܘ ܠܗܘܢ. ܘܠܐ ܐܬܦܠܓܬܘܢ ܒܠܒܐ ܐܢܫܝܢ. ܘܠܐ ܐܒܐܫ ܠܟܘܢ.
7. ܦܩܕ ܡܠܟܐ ܠܐܣܝܪܐ: ܗܦܘܟ ܠܡܕܝܢܬܐ ܘܐܬܐ ܠܗܘܢ ܐܝܟ ܘܫܐܠܗ ܒܫܠܡܗ ܒܦܘܡ.

8. ‏أُسمقنقل ‏ٱهزه ‏: ‏سبَ ‏كم ‏هٔذانْه ‏كي ‏هي ‏شزنئلا ‏اهّلا ‏وهُسكاهَكُم
‏حنيَأا ‏وَاكُهُا ‏.

9. ‏حهّه ‏آحلا ‏هٔاكُه ‏هكلحهُا ‏ةاهِهزهُا ‏. ‏هُكاكي ‏بههّه ‏كُهِزيِيِهُا ‏اُنُه
‏هي ‏هحزٔه ‏وهَلهُ ‏هكهب ‏ونُازْا ‏حهَكلحهةُاُا ‏.

10. ‏خنُ ‏: ‏هُهاكْه ‏هي ‏واهّد ‏اُهَهد ‏اُزههُاُا ‏.

Translate into Syriac:

1. I have not given you (*m. pl.*) the land because you have
done evil in my eyes.   2. If you (*f. pl.*) have done good in
your youth, when you grow old it shall not weary you.
3. If you ask anything in my name, it will be given to you.
4. The servant said to his master, 'It is a small (thing) that I
have asked of you, and you cannot refuse.'   5. She is going
to give me the book for which I asked.   6. Do not be dis-
pleased that I have given food to these people who have
nothing to eat.   7. There was a dispute about the gift and
she declined it.   8. She greeted her father and kissed him.
9. Do (*pl.*) not ask 'Where are you going to go?'   10. Did
God perhaps not know that Cain was going to do evil?

24. HOLLOW VERBS

These verbs are so called because the middle letter of the root is a vowel. Their peculiarities are best explained if this vowel was originally *waw*, and so they are also known as ʿ*e*-*waw* verbs and are listed in dictionaries with this spelling, e.g. ܩܘܡ 'rise, stand'. There are, however, no verbs of this class that show the *waw* in the peʿal perfect.[1]

Hollow verbs, like the ʿ*e-alaph* verbs, start their inflection from a monosyllable. In the peʿal perfect, the vowel of this syllable is always *ā*, except in the verb ܡܝܬ 'die' where it is *i*. In the impf. and imv., the vowel is *u* (not *o* as in the strong verbs) except in the verb ܣܘܡ 'put' where it is *i*.[2] Thus:

	perfect		imperfect	
3rd m. sing.	ܩܡ	ܡܝܬ	ܢܩܘܡ	ܢܣܝܡ
3rd f. sing.	ܩܡܬ	ܡܝܬܬ	ܬܩܘܡ	ܬܣܝܡ
2nd m. sing.	ܩܡܬ	ܡܝܬܬ	ܬܩܘܡ	ܬܣܝܡ
2nd f. sing.	ܩܡܬܝ	ܡܝܬܬܝ	ܬܩܘܡܝܢ	ܬܣܝܡܝܢ
1st sing.	ܩܡܬ	ܡܝܬܬ	ܐܩܘܡ	ܐܣܝܡ
3rd m. pl.	ܩܡܘ	ܡܝܬܘ	ܢܩܘܡܘܢ	ܢܣܝܡܘܢ
3rd f. pl.	ܩܡ	ܡܝܬ	ܢܩܘܡܢ	ܢܣܝܡܢ
2nd m. pl.	ܩܡܬܘܢ	ܡܝܬܬܘܢ	ܬܩܘܡܘܢ	ܬܣܝܡܘܢ
2nd f. pl.	ܩܡܬܝܢ	ܡܝܬܬܝܢ	ܬܩܘܡܢ	ܬܣܝܡܢ
1st pl.	ܩܡܢ	ܡܝܬܢ	ܢܩܘܡ	ܢܣܝܡ

[1] Verbs that actually have a middle letter *waw* in the perfect, such as ܪܘܙ 'rejoice', treat it as a consonant and so are strong verbs.

[2] The root of this verb is sometimes given as ܣܝܡ rather than ܣܘܡ.

Notice in the foregoing paradigm[3] that there is no vowel on
the preformative of the imperfect, except in the 1st sing.

The other forms of the pe‘al are as follows:

imperative		ܩܽܘܡ, ܩܳܡ
infinitive		ܡܩܳܡ
active participle	m.	ܩܳܐܶܡ, pl. ܩܳܝܡܺܝܢ
	f.	ܩܳܝܡܳܐ, pl. ܩܳܝܡܳܢ
passive participle		ܩܺܝܡ

Notice the unexpected *alaph* in the masc. sing. active ptc.
This is dropped in the fem. and pl., which have a *yod*.

In the pa‘el and ethpa‘al, the middle root letter appears as
consonantal *yod*, so that the verbs are conjugated regularly;
e.g. from ܣܘܕ we have ܚܰܝܶܒ 'convict' and its passive ܐܶܬܚܰܝܰܒ.

In the aph‘el pf. and imv. the vowel of the stem is *i* and the
vowel of the preformative *a*. In the aph‘el impf., inf. and
ptcs. there is no vowel on the preformative: this is a difference from all other classes of verb. In the impf., the aph‘el
thus resembles the pe‘al, except that the stem vowel is *i* instead of *u*. The infinitive is the same as the pe‘al except for
the ending ܘ-. The following is the paradigm for the aph‘el:

		sing.	pl.
perfect	3rd m.	ܐܰܩܺܝܡ	ܐܰܩܺܝܡܘ
	3rd f.	ܐܰܩܺܝܡܰܬ	ܐܰܩܺܝܡ
	2nd m.	ܐܰܩܺܝܡܬ	ܐܰܩܺܝܡܬܘܢ
	2nd f.	ܐܰܩܺܝܡܬܝ	ܐܰܩܺܝܡܬܝܢ
	1st	ܐܰܩܺܝܡܶܬ	ܐܰܩܺܝܡܢ

---

[3] The paradigms in this lesson omit the longer forms of the verb.

imperfect	3rd m.	ܢܩܝܡ	ܢܩܝܡܘܢ
	3rd f.	ܬܩܝܡ	ܢܩܝܡܢ
	2nd m.	ܬܩܝܡ	ܬܩܝܡܘܢ
	2nd f.	ܬܩܝܡܝܢ	ܬܩܝܡܢ
	1st	ܐܩܝܡ	ܢܩܝܡ
imperative	m.	ܐܩܝܡ	ܐܩܝܡܘ
	f.	ܐܩܝܡܝ	ܐܩܝܡܝ

infinitive ܡܩܡܘ

participles act. ܡܩܝܡ pass. ܡܩܡ.

The ethpeʿel of hollow verbs properly speaking does not exist, its place being taken by the ettaphʿal,[4] which therefore may be the passive of the peʿal or the aphʿel. It is formed from the aphʿel in the usual way (see pp. 80-1). Thus we have ܐܬܬܩܝܡ (*etqim*) 'he was raised', ܐܬܬܩܝܡܬ (*etqimaṯ*), etc. The two ܬ-s may be reduced to one in spelling, as in ܐܬܩܝܡ (= ܐܬܬܩܝܡ).

The verb ܦܝܣ is a loan-word from Greek πεῖσαι 'persuade'. (The ܦ takes *qushaya* throughout.) It is used in the aphʿel and ettaphʿal only. The aphʿel ܐܦܝܣ can mean 'persuade, convince, instruct, request', and the pass. ptc. ܡܦܣ 'persuaded' or (with ܒ-) 'knowing, acquainted'. The ettaphʿal ܐܬܬܦܝܣ (more usually spelled ܐܬܛܦܝܣ) has the additional meaning of 'consent to, obey'. Examples are:

ܐܦܝܣܢ ܕܠܐ ܢܐܙܠ he persuaded us not to go

[4] This form is, however, called the ethpeʿel in the *Compendious Syriac Dictionary*.

ܘܰܠܚܰܡܕܐ ܠܐ ܐܠܡܗܦܣܡܩ   lest you be disobedient

ܡܕܦܩܡܢ ܚܢܐܡܕܘܦܗܐ   we know the law.

Vocabulary

ܩܘܡ	rise, stand;	ܡܘܬܐ	die
	pa., aph. establish;	ܪܘܡ	be high;
	aph. raise up, set up		*aph.* exalt, lift up
ܣܘܡ	put, lay	ܠܘܛ	curse
ܙܘܥ	shake, move (*intrans.*);	ܕܘܢ	judge
	aph. set in motion	ܚܘܪ	look at (+ܒ-)
ܬܘܒ	repent	ܚܘܒ	owe, be wrong;
ܫܶܬܐܣܬܐ	foundation (*f.*);		*pa.* convict
	pl. ܫܶܬܐܣܐ	ܟܗܢܐ	priest
ܩܪܝܒ	near	ܡܢ ܫܠܝܐ	suddenly
ܩܝܡܐ	covenant	ܐܓܪܐ	wages
ܡܕܒܚܐ	altar	ܐܘܥܐ	movement, quake

Exercises

Translate into English:

١. ܩܥܢܠܐ ܘܚܘܙܢܐ ܐܘܙܥܝܓܐܣ ܐܘܠܠ ܐܝܗܩܐܠ.

٢. ܠܐ ܐܘܕܝܩܢ ܘܠܐ ܐܠܐܙܘܣܩܢ. ܚܝܢܠܐ ܠܝܚܙ ܘܘܥܣܠܝ ܠܝܗܩܢ ܐܠܐܙܘܣܩܢ.

٣. ܘܡܢ ܫܠܝܐ ܐܘܥܐ ܘܟܐ ܗܘܐ؛ ܘܐܠܡܐܢܣܐ ܫܶܬܐܣܐ ܘܚܡ ܐܗܩܢܙܐ ܘܐܠܐܦܐܡܣܗ ܡܣܝܐ ܐܘܬܢܐ ܩܠܚܗܢ.

٤. ܩܪܝܒ ܗܘܐ ܠܓܠܚܢܐ ܠܟܡܥܟܗ ܘܐܩܣܡܗܗ ܐܟܬܗܘܘܗ ܠܚܩܩܢܡܐ ܘܠܟܕܥܪܒܗܘܘܗ ܡܣܝܐ.

٥. ܒ ܗܒܝܢ ܩܘܢܠܐ ܒܪܡ ܡܕܒܚܣܐ ܘܩܐܡ ܘܠܘܩܗܣ ܠܟܗ ܘܡܕܢܥܪ ܩܠܟܗ ܘܐܟܕ ܠܟܪܠܚܦܐܐ ܗܘܙܐ.

Translate into Syriac:

1. Repent, that God may not judge you in his anger.   2. I have laid a foundation, and another foundation than that which is laid, can no one lay.   3. Lift up your heads, o gates, and be lifted (up), you gates that are from eternity.   4. We believe that he who was raised from the dead will also raise us up with him, and will set us at his right hand.   5. You are cursed by the earth which has received the blood of your brother.   6. I am persuaded that I shall not be convicted by the judge.   7. He raised his voice to curse the enemy, but it was a blessing that came out of his mouth.   8. The Lord commanded the Israelites (*lit.* sons of Israel) that they should not set up covenants with the peoples of the land.   9. Are you acquainted with (*use* ܚܡܣ) the writings (*lit.* written things, *f.*) of Mar Ephrem?   10. He is cursed by all who look at him.

25. GEMINATE VERBS

These are verbs in which the second and third root letters
are the same (twins, *gemini*). They are also called *double-ʿe*
verbs. Generally, in those parts where both the second and
third root letters carry vowels, both are written and the verb
is conjugated regularly. Otherwise, the latter root letter is
only written once and the stem becomes a monosyllable. In
dictionaries these verbs are listed (following the 3rd m. sing.
peʿal form) as though they had only two letters in the root.

In the peʿal perfect the stem is monosyllabic and has the
vowel *a*. When the the second root letter is a *bgdkpt* it takes
qushaya (a sign of being doubled) only when it is between
vowels. The following are the forms for ܒܙ 'plunder' and
ܫܒ 'let down':

	sing.	pl.	sing.	pl.
3rd m.	ܒܰܙ	ܒܰܙܘ	ܫܶܒ	ܫܶܒܘ
3rd f.	ܒܶܙܰܬ	ܒܰܙ	ܫܶܒܰܬ	ܫܶܒ
2nd m.	ܒܰܙܬ	ܒܰܙܬܘܢ	ܫܶܒܬ	ܫܶܒܬܘܢ
2nd f.	ܒܰܙܬܝ	ܒܰܙܬܝܢ	ܫܶܒܬܝ	ܫܶܒܬܝܢ
1st	ܒܶܙܶܬ	ܒܰܙܢ	ܫܶܒܶܬ	ܫܶܒܢ

There are the usual longer forms of the 3rd plural. For ܫܒ
these are: m. ܫܶܒܘܢ; f. ܫܶܒܝ, ܫܶܒܶܝܢ

In the peʿal imperfect, the vowel may be *o* or *a*, just as in
the strong verbs. Curiously, the first root letter is doubled:
that is, if a *bgdkpt* it takes *qushaya*, as in the *pe-nun* verbs.
The same happens with the infinitive. Thus:

		sing.	pl.
impf.	3rd m.	ܢܒܘܙ	ܢܒܙܘܢ
	3rd f.	ܬܒܘܙ	ܢܒܙܢ
	2nd m.	ܬܒܘܙ	ܬܒܙܘܢ
	2nd f.	ܬܒܙܝܢ	ܬܒܙܢ
	1st	ܐܒܘܙ	ܢܒܘܙ
imperative	m.	ܒܘܙ	ܒܘܙܘ, ܒܘܙܘܢ
	f.	ܒܘܙܝ	ܒܘܙܝ, ܒܘܙܝܢ
infinitive		ܡܒܙ	

In the peʿal active participle, an *alaph* is inserted in the masculine singular (as in the hollow verbs) and sometimes in the plural also. Thus:

active ptc.	m.	ܒܐܙ, pl. ܒܙܝܢ or ܒܐܙܝܢ
	f.	ܒܐܙܐ, pl. ܒܙܢ
passive ptc.		ܒܙܝܙ

The ethpeʿel is regular except that in forms where the two geminated letters have no full vowel between them, only one of them may be written. Thus:

ethpeʿel	pf.	ܐܬܒܙܙ, ܐܬܒܙܙܬ or ܐܬܒܙܬ, ܐܬܒܙܙܬ, etc.
	impf.	ܢܬܒܙܙ, ܬܬܒܙܙܝܢ or ܬܬܒܙܝܢ, etc.

In the aphʿel the first root letter is again doubled as in the *pe-nun* verbs. Thus:

aphʿel	pf.	ܐܒܙ, ܐܒܙܬ, ܐܒܙܬ, etc.
	impf.	ܢܒܙ, ܬܒܙܝܢ, ܢܒܙܘܢ, etc.
	imv.	ܐܒܙ, ܐܒܙܘ, etc.; ܐܒܙܘܢ, ܐܒܙܝܢ

Some geminate verbs have a palpel and an ethpalpal conjugation. For example from ܒܠ we have ܒܰܠܒܶܠ 'confuse' and ܐܶܬܒܰܠܒܰܠ 'be confused'. These are conjugated like other quadriliteral verbs (§16).

Vocabulary

ܒܰܙ	plunder, *o*	ܫܰܒ	let down, *o*
ܓܰܫ	touch, *o*	ܟܣܣ	*aph*. reprove;
ܚܰܒ	*aph*. love		*ethp*. be reproved
ܚܰܢ	show mercy (to), *o*	ܦܣܣ	*aph*. permit[1]
ܥܰܠ	enter, *o*	ܚܰܫ	suffer, *a*
ܫܰܪ	be proved true;	ܒܠ	*palpel* confuse
	aph. confirm	ܒܗܬ	be ashamed, *a*
ܚܰܒܺܝܒ	beloved	ܢܶܣܝܽܘܢܳܐ	temptation
ܚܰܣܺܝܢ	strong	ܣܽܘܥܪܳܢܳܐ	thing, matter
ܫܽܘܪܳܐ	wall	ܐܶܣܦܪܺܝܕܳܐ	basket
ܓܰܪܡܳܐ	bone	ܪ̈ܰܚܡܶܐ	mercy (*pl.*)
ܡܳܐܢܳܐ	vessel, garment, possession	ܫܝܽܘܠ	Sheol (*f.*)

Exercises

Translate into English:

1. ܗܳܠܶܝܢ ܐܽܘܪ̈ܚܳܐ ܕܡܳܪܝܳܐ ܕܙܰܕܺܝ̈ܩܶܐ ܐܳܙܠܺܝܢ ܒܗܶܝܢ.

2. ܐܰܚܒܽܘ ܕܐܶܢܳܐ ܐܰܚܶܒܬܟܽܘܢ: ܐܳܦ ܐܰܢ̱ܬܽܘܢ ܐܰܚܶܒܘ ܚܰܕ ܠܚܰܕ.

3. ܚܰܘܢܝ ܕܚܰܣܺܝܢܳܐ ܥܰܠ ܚܛܳܗ̈ܝ ܘܥܰܠܡܰܝ̈ ܪ̈ܰܚܡܶܐ ܡܶܢ ܐܰܠܳܗܳܐ ܡܳܪܳܐ ܟܽܠ.

[1] Not to be confused with ܦܘܫ (§24).

4. ܐܡܰܪ ܢܒܝܐ ܠܡܠܟܐ ܡܛܠ ܕܐܝܬ ܠܗ܂ ܐܢܬܬܐ ܕܐܚܘܗܝ ܢܣܒ ܚܒܪܐ ܘܟܐܢܬܐ
ܟܠܗ ܟܠܗ܂

5. ܐܚܒ ܠܒܥܠܕܒܒܝܟܘܢ ܘܗܘܝܬܘܢ܂ ܢܛܪ ܠܐ ܡܢܩܦܝܢ ܠܐܝܠܝܢ ܠܡܨܚܟܝܢ ܚܢܐ܂

6. ܐܢ ܠܟ ܡܢܩܦ ܐܢܫ܂ ܐܦܝܣ ܠܟܡ ܡܬܓܠܐ ܠܢܫܐ ܘܫܢܝܢܐ ܗܢܐ܂

7. ܐܚܬܝܬܐ ܘܗܘܝܬܘܢ ܗܘܝܢܘܢ ܕܐܫܚܙܒܐ ܘܡܚܙܚܘܢ ܥܠ ܗܦܘܐ܂

8. ܠܐ ܡܥܠ ܠܟܡܠܐ ܘܐܦܩ ܡܬܡܐ ܗܝܢܬܐ܂ ܘܗܦܠܐ ܐܘܩܨܗ
ܘܐܠܥܨܟ ܘܗܠܟܨܢܝ ܘܟܠܝܠܗ ܐܗܢܝ ܗܘܗ܂

9. ܐܡܩܠܐ ܐܝܠܘܢ ܡܗܩܝܣ ܘܠܕܒܠܐ ܠܟܬܡܐ ܥܩܩܠܐ ܘܗܘܠܬܢܘܢ ܢܚܕ ܐܠܐ ܐܢ
ܠܕܥܡܝ̈ܡ ܠܐܗܙܡܘܘܢ ܠܟܬܩܩܠܐ܂

10. ܦܚܚܡ ܠܟܡ ܡܚܙܚܚ ܠܐ ܐܡܪ ܘܐܟܚܚܟܠܐ ܠܚܡܦܚܢܘܢ ܐܠܐ ܘܐܡܗܙ ܠܟܡ
ܠܠܟܡܘܘܢ ܚܣ ܢܟܠܨܐ ܐܗܟܝ܂

Translate into Syriac:

1. The prophet reproved the king because he had taken his brother's wife. 2. Love your enemies and be merciful (*use* ܚܢ) to those who curse you. 3. The apostle said, I do not permit women to teach. 4. If one (*use* ܐܢܫ) suffers as a Christian let him not be ashamed. 5. The holy vessels cannot be touched. It is not permitted to touch them. 6. God confused all their languages. 7. The emperor sent his soldiers to plunder the city, and to show no mercy. 8. The apostle wrote to confirm the faith of his disciples. 9. Where is it written that the messiah should (*use* ܠܡ) suffer? 10. Do not bring us into (*use the aph. of* ܥܠ) temptation.

26. LAMAD-YOD VERBS, I: THE PEᶜAL

This is a large class of verbs, including many common ones. They diverge the furthest from the strong verbs because the weak final letter of the root has interacted with the inflectional endings. These verbs usually appear in dictionaries as if the last root letter were *alaph*, and so the quoted form is in most cases the 3rd m. singular, e.g. ܓܒܐ 'he chose'. But in this form the *alaph* is really only a vowel letter taking the place of an original *yod*.[1]

In the peᶜal perfect there are the usual two different conjugations originally corresponding to transitive and intransitive verbs; but in *lamad-yod* verbs these two look more different from each other than usual. In the transitive-type verbs, like ܓܒܐ, the third radical letter *yod* does not appear at all in the 3rd m. or f. sing. or 3rd m. pl. In the intransitive-type verbs, like ܫܠܐ 'be quiet', the *yod* is a consonant *y* in the 3rd f. sing. and otherwise a vowel *i*. The full paradigm is as follows:

	sing.	pl.	sing.	pl.
3rd m.	ܓܒܐ	ܓܒܘ	ܫܠܝ	ܫܠܝܘ
3rd f.	ܓܒܬ	ܓܒܝ	ܫܠܝܬ	ܫܠܝ
2nd m.	ܓܒܝܬ	ܓܒܝܬܘܢ	ܫܠܝܬ	ܫܠܝܬܘܢ
2nd f.	ܓܒܝܬܝ	ܓܒܝܬܝܢ	ܫܠܝܬܝ	ܫܠܝܬܝܢ
1st	ܓܒܝܬ	ܓܒܝܢ	ܫܠܝܬ	ܫܠܝܢ

[1] The few genuinely *lamad-alaph* verbs, like ܒܝܐ 'console' and ܛܠܐ 'soil', all paᶜels, behave like strong verbs with a final guttural.

There are in addition longer forms for the 1st pl., ܓܒܝܢܢ and ܫܠܝܢܢ, which are common. Longer forms for the 3rd pl. ܓܒܐܘܢ and ܓܒܝ̈ܢ are less common.

Notice the 3rd pl. forms, which have differences from all the other classes of verb. In the masc., the ending ܘ- is pronounced: ܓܒܘ *g̱baw* and ܫܠܝܘ *šliw*. The fem. pl. ܓܒܝ̈ is not the same as the 3rd m. sing. and it is written with *seyame*.

In the imperfect, the transitive and intransitive types come together. The following is the conjugation of ܓܒܐ, but for ܫܠܐ the forms are just the same: ܢܫܠܐ etc.

	sing.	pl.
3rd masc.	ܢܓܒܐ	ܢܓܒܘܢ
3rd fem.	ܬܓܒܐ	ܢܓܒܝ̈ܢ
2nd masc.	ܬܓܒܐ	ܬܓܒܘܢ
2nd fem.	ܬܓܒܝܢ	ܬܓܒܝ̈ܢ
1st	ܐܓܒܐ	ܢܓܒܐ

Notice that the ending on the 2nd and 3rd m. pl. is *-on*, not *-un* as in the other classes of verbs.

The imperative is as follows:

masc.	ܓܒܝ	ܓܒܘ
fem.	ܓܒܝ	ܓܒܝ̈ܢ

There is also a longer form of the m. pl.: ܓܒܐܘܢ.

Among the participles, the m. sing. ends in ܐ-. In the other forms a *yod* appears. As with other verbs, the active participle has an invariable vowel *ā* on the first syllable. The passive participle differs from the active only in not having this vowel. Thus we have:

active ptc.	m.	ܡܷܬ݂ܚܙܶܐ	ܡܷܬ݂ܚܙܶܐ
	f.		
passive ptc.	m.		
	f.		

The most usual contracted forms of active participle + enclitic pronoun (the 'present tense', pp. 46-7) are:

2nd m.		
2nd f.		
1st m.		
1st f.		

The following are the declined forms of the passive participle ܓܒ݂ܶܐ 'chosen':

	masc. sing.	pl.	fem. sing.	pl.
abs.				
emph.				
const.				

The active participle has just the same endings, but it has the vowel *ā* on the first syllable throughout. For ܓܒ݂ܶܐ 'choosing' we therefore have emph. ܓܳܒ݂ܝܳܐ, cstr. ܓܳܒ݂ܶܐ; pl. emph. ܓܳܒ݂ܰܝܳܐ, cstr. ܓܳܒ݂ܰܝ, etc.

The infinitive of *lamad-yod* verbs ends in ʾ-, e.g. ܡܷܓ݂ܒܳܐ.

Usage. The verb ܗܘܐ has some idiomatic uses. (1) In dependent clauses, the impf. of any verb can be replaced by the impf. of ܗܘܐ followed by the active participle, as in

ܦܩܰܕܘ ܐܷܢܘܿܢ ܕܠܳܐ ܢܷܗܘܘܿܢ ܡܡܰܠܠܝܼܢ
ܒܫܡܳܐ ܕܝܼܫܘܿܥ.

They commanded them not to speak in the name of Jesus.

(2) The 2nd person pf. of ܗܘܐ before an adjective or participle can have the force of a command or wish:

ܗܘܝܬ ܚܠܝܡܐ farewell (*lit.* be well)
ܗܘܝܬܘܢ ܝܕܥܝܢ ܕ … you should know that …

Vocabulary

ܚܙܐ	see	ܗܘܐ	be, become
ܒܢܐ	build	ܚܕܐ or ܚܕܝ	rejoice
ܩܪܐ	call, read	ܓܒܐ	choose
ܒܥܐ	ask for, seek, require	ܣܢܐ	hate
ܨܒܐ	wish, want	ܥܢܐ	answer
ܚܠܡ	*pass. ptc.* well, whole; *ethp.* be made well	ܚܶܠܩܳܐ	fate
		ܫܠܐ	be quiet, cease
ܨܥܪܐ	disgrace	ܥܣܘ	Esau
ܒܝܪܬܐ	fortress, palace	ܙܘܙܐ	coin
ܝܗܘܕܐ	Judas[2]	ܥܘܠܐ	wrong, injustice

Exercises

Translate into English:

1. ܠܐ ܐܝܬ ܠܝ ܚܠܩܐ ܠܡܥܒܕ ܡܕܡ ܟܕ ܠܐ ܨܒܝܢ.
2. ܡܢܘ ܗܘ ܕܢܓܒܐ ܠܗ ܨܥܪܐ ܚܠܦ ܐܝܩܪܐ ܐܘ ܡܘܬܐ ܚܠܦ ܚܝܐ.
3. ܐܡܪ ܡܠܟܐ ܠܝܗܘܕܐ: ܗܫܐ ܨܒܐ ܐܢܐ ܕܬܒܢܐ ܠܝ ܒܝܪܬܐ. ܐܡܪ ܠܗ ܝܗܘܕܐ ܗܟܢܐ ܠܐ ܡܫܟܚ ܐܢܐ ܠܡܒܢܝܘ ܒܗܢܐ ܐܬܪܐ. ܐܡܪ ܠܗ ܡܠܟܐ: ܘܒܐܝܢܐ ܐܬܪܐ ܡܫܟܚ ܐܢܬ ܠܡܒܢܝܘ.

[2] The proper name of Thomas in the Syriac *Acts of Thomas*.

Translate into Syriac:

1. And the word became flesh and we saw its glory. 2. Sir, I ask that you should see my son, who is ill. 3. If you wish to learn, follow (*use* ܢܩܦ) a good teacher. 4. He said to the wind, 'Be quiet.' And it was quiet. 5. We cannot see those (things) that are (*use* ܚܕܡ) to be. 6. Judas built the king a heavenly palace instead of the one he asked for. 7. When they read the names of the chosen, I rejoiced to hear mine. 8. The judge wanted to call the woman before him, but no one could find her. 9. The faith is built upon the foundation of the gospel. 10. She was made well, and returned to her house (*use* ܠ) rejoicing.

27. LAMAD-YOD VERBS, 2: OTHER CONJUGATIONS

Lamad-yod verbs have similarities across all the other conjugations (ethpeʿel, ethpaʿal, aphʿel, and ettaphʿal). In the perfect, these verbs have the same endings as the peʿal of the intransitive-type verbs (like ܡܠܟ). In the imperfect and participles, again, all the endings are the same as those of the peʿal. This is also the case with the imperatives except in the m. sing., which ends in ܝ- in the ethpeʿel and otherwise in ܐ-. The infinitives all end in ܝܘ-.

These remarks may be illustrated by the following paradigm for the verb ܓܒܐ. (Only the paʿel is given in full.)

Paʿel perfect	sing.	pl.
3rd m.	ܓܒܝ	ܓܒܝܘ (*gabiw*)
3rd f.	ܓܒܝܬ	ܓܒܝ
2nd m.	ܓܒܝܬ	ܓܒܝܬܘܢ
2nd f.	ܓܒܝܬܝ	ܓܒܝܬܝܢ
1st	ܓܒܝܬ	ܓܒܝܢ
imperfect		
3rd m.	ܢܓܒܐ	ܢܓܒܘܢ
3rd f.	ܬܓܒܐ	ܢܓܒܝܢ
2nd m.	ܬܓܒܐ	ܬܓܒܘܢ
2nd f.	ܬܓܒܝܢ	ܬܓܒܝܢ
1st	ܐܓܒܐ	ܢܓܒܐ
imperative		
m.	ܓܒܐ	ܓܒܘ
f.	ܓܒܝ	ܓܒܝܢ

infinitive		ܡܶܬܚܰܟ̇ܡܳܐ	
participles active	m.	ܡܶܬܚܰܟ̇ܛܳܐ	ܡܶܬܚܰܟ̇ܚܡ
	f.	ܡܶܬܚܰܟ̇ܚܡܳܐ	ܡܶܬܚܰܟ̇ܚܦ
passive	m.	ܡܶܬܚܰܟ̇ܟܳܐ	ܡܶܬܚܰܟ̇ܚܡ
	f.	ܡܶܬܚܰܟ̇ܚܡܳܐ	ܡܶܬܚܰܟ̇ܚܦ

Notice that the active and passive participles are indistinguishable except in the masc. singular. The endings for the declined forms of these participles are just the same as those of the peʿal (§26); thus e.g., ܡܶܬܦܰܪܩܺܝܢ 'those who are delivered'.

Ethpeʿel: pf. ܐܶܬܚܟܺܝܬ, impf. ܢܶܬܚܟܶܐ, , inf. ܡܶܬܚܟܳܝܽܘ, imv. m. ܐܶܬܚܟܰܝ f. ܐܶܬܚܟܳܝ, ptc. ܡܶܬܚܟܶܐ.

Ethpaʿal: pf. ܐܶܬܚܰܟܺܝܬ, impf. ܢܶܬܚܰܟܶܐ, ptc. ܡܶܬܚܰܟܶܐ, imv. ܐܶܬܚܰܟܰܝ.

Aphʿel: pf. ܐܚܟܺܝܬ, impf. ܢܰܚܟܶܐ, active ptc. ܡܰܚܟܶܐ, passive ptc. ܡܰܚܟܰܝ, imv. ܐܰܚܟܳܐ.

Ettaphʿal: pf. ܐܶܬܬܰܚܟܺܝܬ, impf. ܢܶܬܬܰܚܟܶܐ, imv. ܐܶܬܬܰܚܟܳܝܽܘ, etc.

The verb ܐܶܬܐ 'come' is pe-alaph (§21) as well as lamad-yod. The peʿal impf. is ܢܺܐܬܶܐ; imperative m. ܐܳܬܳܐ f. ܐܳܬܳܝ; inf. ܡܶܐܬܳܐ; aphʿel ('bring') pf. ܐܰܝܬܺܝ, impf. ܢܰܝܬܶܐ, imv. ܐܰܝܬܳܐ, inf. ܡܰܝܬܳܝܽܘ.

The verb ܚܝܳܐ 'live' also has some irregular forms. The impf. is ܢܺܚܶܐ (less commonly ܢܶܚܶܐ) or ܢܺܚܶܐ; the imv. m. ܚܺܝ, f. ܚܳܝ, etc.; inf. ܡܶܚܳܐ or ܡܶܚܳܝܽܘ, ptc. ܚܳܝܶܐ. The aphʿel ('give life to, save') has the pf. ܐܰܚܺܝ, ܐܰܚܺܝܬ, ܐܰܚܝܺ, etc.; impf. ܢܰܚܶܐ or ܢܰܚܶܐ; imv. ܐܰܚܳܐ, inf. ܡܰܚܳܝܽܘ; active ptc. ܡܰܚܶܐ or ܡܰܚܝܳܐ; passive ptc. ܡܰܚܝܰܝ.

The verb ܫܪܳܐ in the paʿel means 'begin' (curiously opposite to one meaning of the peʿal, 'come to rest'). It can be

peʿal dwell, live
peʿal loosen, let go

followed by a participle, as in ܫܪܝ ܡܡܠܠ 'he began to speak', equivalent to ܫܪܝ ܠܡܡܠܠܘ or ܫܪܝ ܕܢܡܠܠ.

Vocabulary

ܐܬܐ come; *aph*. bring
ܕܡܐ be like; *pa*. liken
ܨܠܐ *pa*. pray
ܫܪܐ loose, settle, come to rest; *pa*. begin
ܚܘܐ *pa*. show
ܝܕܐ *aph*. confess, thank
ܩܘܐ *pa*. remain, last
ܡܠܐ fill
ܪܥܐ *ethp*. be pleased, consent
ܚܕܘܬܐ joy, rejoicing (*f*.)
ܒܥܘܬܐ petition (*f*.)

ܚܝܐ live; *aph*. save
ܦܨܐ *pa*. save, deliver
ܫܘܐ be worthy, equal; *ethp*. be made worthy
ܚܙܐ *ethp*. appear
ܪܡܐ *aph*. put, cast, throw
ܒܪܐ create; ܒܪܘܝܐ creator
ܕܟܐ or ܕܟܝ be pure; *pa*. purify
ܚܙܘܐ vision, appearance
ܡܚܝܢܐ saving, life-giving
ܙܪܥܐ seed
ܘܝ woe

Exercises

Translate into English:

1. ܡܢ ܕܨܒܐ ܓܒܪ ܕܢܐܬܐ ܢܦܩܘܢ ܢܘܒܠܘܢܝܗ. ܘܡܢ ܕܢܘܒܠ ܢܦܩܘܢ ܡܫܠܛܝܢ ܢܡܚܝܘܢܝܗ ܘܢܚܐ.

2. ܡܘܕܝܢܢ ܚܢܢ ܐܠܗܐ: ܐܒܐ ܐܚܝܕ ܟܠ: ܒܪܘܝܐ ܕܟܠܗܘܢ ܐܝܠܝܢ ܕܡܬܚܙܝܢ ܘܕܠܐ ܡܬܚܙܝܢ.

3. ܚܕܘܬܐ ܥܬܝܕܐ ܠܫܘܝܐ. ܐܠܐ ܘܝ ܠܗܘܢ ܕܒܐܝܕܗ ܐܬܝܐ.

4. ܫܪܝ ܡܚܘܐ ܠܬܠܡܝܕܘܗܝ ܕܙܕܩ ܗܘ ܕܢܐܙܠ ܠܐܘܪܫܠܡ ܘܣܓܝܐܬܐ ܢܚܫ.

Translate into Syriac:

1. She began to read.   2. At that time the city had not been built.   3. Remain here and I will come to you.   4. They laid their hands on the apostles and threw them into prison (*use the aph. of* ܪܡܐ *for both verbs*).   5. He likened the kingdom to a man who had servants.   6. Bring your petitions before God.   7. The priest prays that he should be made worthy to offer the sacrifice.   8. I have come because I want to ask for a blessing from the saint.   9. It is not required of us that we should read the whole book.   10. Be pleased, sir, to accept this gift.

28. PRONOMINAL SUFFIXES ATTACHED
TO LAMAD-YOD VERBS

Suffixes are attached in the ordinary way to forms of these
verbs that end in consonants. With forms that end in vowels, however, there are some variations. It will be easiest to
show these by examples, taking each case in turn.

form	*method of attachment; examples*
any form ending in a consonant	The connecting vowel is as usual.
	ܣܵܐܡܠܝܘܗܝ we saw him
	ܓܒܵܬܗ she chose him
	ܢܸܓܒܘܢܢܝ let them choose me.
pf. ending in ܐ-	The *alaph* is dropped and the *ā* be- comes the connecting vowel.
	ܩܪܵܝܗܝ he called him
	ܣܵܐܡܟ he saw you (*m.*)
	ܣܵܐܡܟܝ he saw you (*f.*).
pf. ending in ܗ-	An *alaph* is inserted and the connec- ting vowel is *u*.
	ܣܵܐܘܟܘܢ they saw you (*m. sing.*)
	ܓܒܵܐܘܗܝ (*gba'u*) they chose him
	ܣܵܐܘܟܝܢ they saw you (*f. pl.*).
pf. ending in ܝ-	The *yod* becomes a consonant and the suffixes are attached as usual.
	ܚܘܝܢܝ (*ḥawyan*) he showed me
	ܘܕܡܝܗ (*damyeh*) he likened it

ܐܲܝܬܝܹܗ (*aytyeh*) he brought him

except for the 2nd pls., which are:

ܚܵܘܝܼܟ݂ܘܿܢ, ܚܵܘܝܼܟ݂ܘܿܢ he showed you.

pf. ending in ܝ-   The connecting vowel *ā* is added.

ܚܙܲܝܵܢ (*ḥzayān*) they (*f.*) saw us

ܚܙܲܝܵܝܗܝ (*ḥzayāy*) they (*f.*) saw him

ܚܵܘܝܵܝܗܝ (*ḥawyāy*) they (*f.*) showed it.

pf. ending in ܘ-   The *yod* becomes a consonant and
the connecting vowel is *u*.

ܚܵܘܝܘܿܗܝ (*ḥawyu*) they showed it

ܐܲܝܬܝܘܢ (*aytyun*) they brought us.

impf. ending in ܐ-   The *alaph* is dropped and *e* becomes
the connecting vowel, written ܶ .

ܢܸܩܪܹܟ݂ (*neqrek*) he will call you

ܢܸܓܠܹܘܗܝ (*neglew*) let us reveal it

ܬܚܵܘܹܝܗ݁ she will show it (*f.*).

imperative   The attachment resembles that for
the perfect, but there are some differences. This is the paradigm:

	m. sing. pe'al	pa'el	fem. sing.	masc. pl.	fem. pl.
no suffix	ܚܙܝ	ܚܲܟ݁ܐ	ܚܙܝ	ܚܙܘ	ܚܙܝܢ
1st sing.	ܚܙܝܢ	ܚܲܟ݁ܝܢ	ܚܲܟ݁ܐܝܢ	ܚܲܟ݁ܐܘܢ	ܚܙܝܢܝܢ
3rd m. sg.	ܚܙܝܘܗܝ	ܚܲܟ݁ܝܘܗܝ	ܚܲܟ݁ܐܝܘܗܝ	ܚܲܟ݁ܐܘܘܗܝ	ܚܙܝܢܝܘܗܝ
3rd f. sg.	ܚܙܝܗ	ܚܲܟ݁ܗ	ܚܲܟ݁ܐܗ	ܚܲܟ݁ܐܘܗ	ܚܙܝܢܗ
1st pl.	ܚܙܝܢ	ܚܲܟ݁ܢ	ܚܲܟ݁ܐܢ	ܚܲܟ݁ܐܢ	ܚܙܝܢܢ

infinitive
In the pe'al, the *yod* of the root appears as a consonant, to which suffixes are attached as usual:

ܡܚܣܝܬܗ to see him

ܡܩܪܝܢܝ to call me.

In other conjugations, the attachment is to the ـܝܳܐ- form as usual:

ܡܣܝܡܳܝܐܗ to put it.

Usage. Syriac does not always distinguish what in English are direct and indirect objects of verbs. (Notice how -ܠ can indicate either of these.) Accordingly, the objective pronominal suffixes are sometimes used for indirect objects, as in:

ܐܠܦܝܢ ܠܡܨܠܝܘ teach us to pray

ܐܚܘܝܘܗܝ ܢܦܫܝ I will show myself to him.

Vocabulary

ܟܣܝ	*pa.* hide, cover	ܠܘܐ	*pa.* accompany
ܓܠܝ	reveal, make clear	ܡܚܐ	strike, beat
ܨܒܝܢܐ	will, wish	ܩܕܫ	*pa.* sanctify
ܐܪܙܐ	mystery	ܟܪܡܐ	vineyard
ܣܗܕܘ	martyr (*m.*)	ܟܠܝܠܐ	crown
ܚܘܒܐ	debt, sin	ܣܢܝܩܘܬܐ	need
ܚܝܒ	indebted, guilty	ܚܡܪܐ	(male) donkey
ܛܘܒܘ	happy are	ܡܫܡܫܢܐ	minister, deacon
	(+ *sfx.*+ -ܠ)	ܕܝܬܩܐ	testament (*f.*)

Exercises

Translate into English:

١. ܡܶܢܗܽܘܢ ܘܰܣܐܝܢܗܽܘܢ ܗܶܢܽܘܢ܆ ܠܗܽܘܟܬܘܡܦ ܠܠܐܣܟܝ ܘܠܐ ܣܐܪܐܦܣ ܗܶܣܘܡܗܶܢܘ.

٢. ܪܶܟܬ ܥܰܚܬܝܐܗ ܟܡܗܟܗܣܐܗ܆ ܗܶܢ ܘܶܒ ܐܗܡܐܪܟܗ ܘܐܡܕܙܐ܆ ܠܐ ܐܢܠ ܗܬܗܦܣܠ ܘܐܐܠܠܐ ܟܠܣܗܘܒܢ.

٣. ܘܗܡܕܙܐ ܟܙܢܗܠ ܗܳܒܙܽܘ ܠܚܕܙܗܘܗܘ܆ ܗܐܣ ܘܗܣܡܐܗܘܗܘ ܗܐܣ ܘܗܓܗܠܟܗܘܘ܆ ܗܗܳܒܙܽܘ ܠܗܘܗ ܠܟܗܙ̄ܗ܆ ܗܟܪ ܣܐܪܐܦܗܘܗ ܐܘܗܡܗܘܗ ܠܚܟܙ ܗܢ ܟܙܢܗܠ.

٤. ܠܐ ܚܟܡܗܗܢܣ ܐܢܠ ܐܢܠ ܚܟܡܗܣܗܢ ܘܐܗܗܗܢ ܗܶܣܗܡܝ ܩܐܙܐ.

٥. ܢܶܠܐ ܗܗܢܠ ܘܐܢܐ ܘܗܚܗܗܟܗ ܗܶܢ ܗܰܟܢܗܠܐ ܐܣܝ ܘܐܗܟܙ ܗܟܠܣܢܐ܆ ܗܡܗܠ ܘܗܢܗܟܗܣ ܐܢܠ ܐܩܣܗܗܝ.

٦. ܗܶܡ ܗܘܗܘܐ ܗܗܩܶܢܠ ܙܶܟܬ܆ ܘܗܘܗܕ ܠܟ ܗܢܶܝ ܗܟܠܠ ܗܗܢܠ܆ ܡܶܢܗܠܐ ܘܓܚܟܠܢܐ ܗܘܣ ܟܗܡ ܘܐܢܠ ܗܢܗܟܐܗ ܡܶܢܗܠܐ ܘܘܗܫܗܡܕܐܝ ܗܚܟܠܟܗ ܢܶܗܡܣ ܗܶܡܶܢܬ ܘܐܣܐܡܝ ܘܐܣܬܙܐ.

٧. ܥܶܗܠܣ ܐܘ ܗܶܟܠܗܟܢܠ ܢܶܠܐ ܢܶܡܗܶܣ ܟܙ ܠܝ ܐܣܗܠ ܐܗܟܙ ܗܗܡܕܟܐ ܘܠܶܗܶܗܕ ܐܝܗܡܐܐ ܘܐܘܗܟܡ ܗܢܬܙܐ.

٨. ܡܢܗܟܗܡ ܗܶܢ ܦܟܗܗ ܠܟܗܣ ܗܶܢܙܢܐ܆ ܠܢܠܣܶܣ ܘܐܠܗܶܗ ܗܘܩܒܙܐܶܣܡ.

٩. ܗܘܗܘܘܢܶܟ ܠܠܟܠܗܘܐ ܘܐܗܗܶܣ ܘܠܢܗܗܐ ܗܗܡܶܢܬܗܦܗܠܐ ܘܘܘܬܟܐܗܡܠ ܣܶܙܐܐܠ܆ ܠܐ ܚܗܗܗܟܐ ܐܢܠ ܚܙܗܢܣܠ܆ ܗܗܡܕܟܐ ܠܝܗܙ ܗܽܡܙ ܗܽܗܢܠܐ܆ ܘܘܗܢܠ ܘܶܒ ܗܶܣܢܠܐ.

١٠. ܗܘܗܩܢܠ ܗܘܗܣܠܐ ܙܶܟܬ ܐܝܶܗܦ܆ ܐܚܗܦ ܘܚܗܡܗܟܢܠ܆ ܠܚܗܗܒܙܶܗ ܗܶܡܗܝ܆ ܐܐܢܐܐ ܗܶܟܠܗܗܗܐܡܝ܆ ܢܗܗܐ ܗܙܗܘܢܠܘ܆ ܐܣܗܟܢܠ ܘܚܗܡܗܟܢܠ ܐܦ ܟܐܘܢܟܢܠ܆ ܗܗܕ ܠܟ ܠܟܣܗܟܢܠ ܘܗܡܗܘܢܗܩܢܝ ܗܘܡܗܢܢܠ܆ ܗܡܗܗܗܦ ܠܟ ܗܶܗܗܟܝ܆ ܐܣܗܟܢܠ ܘܐܦ ܣܝܬ ܗܟܗܡ ܠܚܶܣܬܗܟܝ܆ ܘܠܠ ܐܶܟܠܟ ܠܚܢܗܡܗܗܢܠ܆ ܐܢܠ ܩܶܗܝ ܗܶܢ ܟܶܣܗܠܐ. ܡܶܢܗܠܐ ܘܘܣܠܟܝ ܗܘܣ ܗܶܟܠܗܗܐܐܠ ܗܶܣܠܐ ܘܐܗܚܗܢܣܐ̈ܐ ܠܟܢܟܟܗ ܢܗܟܠܗܡܝ.

Translate into Syriac:

1. You (*sing.*) have come into the light and the light has revealed you. 2. Unto what shall I liken you, o daughter of Jerusalem? 3. God chose you out of all the nations. 4. The priest brought the book before the king and read it to him. 5. He who has seen me has seen the Father, and how can you say, 'Reveal him to me'? 6. She took the coin, looked at it, and threw it on the ground. 7. When you find the donkey, loose (ܫܪܝ) it and bring it to me.   8. No one knew this mystery. God hid it from human beings. 9. Moses was commanded to strike the rock, and he struck it.   10. He left the city with his friend who accompanied him on his way.

29. NUMBERS

The numbers in Syriac are nouns, standing in apposition to the nouns to which they are attached. The object numbered is in the plural (except after ܚܲܕ, ܚܕܳܐ 'one').

The cardinal numbers from 1 to 19 have two forms, one used with masculine nouns and one with feminine. These are as follows:

	with m.	with f.		with m.	with f.
1	ܚܲܕ	ܚܕܳܐ	11	ܚܕܲܥܣܲܪ	ܚܕܲܥܣܸܪ̈ܐ
2	ܬܪܹܝܢ	ܬܲܪ̈ܬܹܝܢ	12	ܬܪܲܥܣܲܪ	ܬܲܪܬܲܥܣܸܪ̈ܐ
3	ܬܠܳܬܳܐ	ܬܠܳܬ	13	ܬܠܳܬܲܥܣܲܪ	ܬܠܳܬܲܥܣܸܪ̈ܐ
4	ܐܲܪ̈ܒܥܳܐ	ܐܲܪܒܲܥ	14	ܐܲܪܒܲܥܣܲܪ	ܐܲܪܒܲܥܣܸܪ̈ܐ
5	ܚܲܡܫܳܐ	ܚܲܡܸܫ	15	ܚܲܡܫܲܥܣܲܪ	ܚܲܡܫܲܥܣܸܪ̈ܐ
6	ܫܬܳܐ, ܐܸܫܬܳܐ	ܫܸܬ	16	ܫܬܲܥܣܲܪ	ܫܬܲܥܣܸܪ̈ܐ
7	ܫܲܒܥܳܐ	ܫܒܲܥ	17	ܫܒܲܥܣܲܪ	ܫܒܲܥܣܸܪ̈ܐ
8	ܬܡܳܢܝܳܐ	ܬܡܳܢܹܐ	18	ܬܡܳܢܲܥܣܲܪ	ܬܡܳܢܲܥܣܸܪ̈ܐ
9	ܬܸܫܥܳܐ	ܬܫܲܥ	19	ܬܫܲܥܣܲܪ	ܬܫܲܥܣܸܪ̈ܐ
10	ܥܸܣܪܳܐ	ܥܣܲܪ			

Notice the forms that take *seyame*: both forms of 'two' and otherwise just the with-feminine forms above ten.[1]

The number usually precedes the noun that is numbered, and in this case, the noun is in the absolute state. Thus: ܬܠܳܬܳܐ ܓܲܒܪ̈ܝܼܢ 'three men'. If the noun should come first, it is

---

[1] But in manuscripts there is a great deal of variation in the use of *seyame* with numbers.

more likely to be in the emphatic, as in ܡܢܝ̈ܢ ܐܡܿܢܬܥܣܪ̈ 'eighteen years'.

There are some special forms of numbers that are nouns.

a. To express a day of the month, the ܝܠ- ending may be added to the simplest form of the number, e.g., ܚܡܫܬܝܠܐ 'on the fifth [day of the month]'.

b. A similar form is used for such other expressions as ܬܪܥܣܪ̈ܬܐ 'the Twelve'.

c. Numbers can occur with the suffixes -ܗܘܢ and -ܗܝܢ. For 'two' there are masculine and feminine forms ܬܪ̈ܝܗܘܢ, ܬܪ̈ܬܝܗܝܢ 'the two of them'; for the rest, the number is invariable, e.g. ܬܠܬܝܗܘܢ or ܬܠܬܝܗܝܢ ' the three of them'. The other forms up to ten are: ܬܪ̈ܝܗܘܢ/ܐܪ̈ܒܥܬܝܗܘܢ, ܚܡܫܬܝܗܘܢ, ܫܬܬܝܗܘܢ, ܫܒܥܬܝܗܘܢ, ܬܡܢܝܬܝܗܘܢ, ܐܫܬܥܬܝܗܘܢ, ܬܫܥܬܝܗܘܢ, ܥܣܪ̈ܬܝܗܘܢ. Note the hard pronunciation of the tau-s. Seyame seems to be optional in these forms.

For the numbers 20-90 there is only one form:

20	ܥܣܪ̈ܝܢ	60	ܫܬܝܢ or ܐܫܬܝܢ
30	ܬܠܬܝܢ	70	ܫܒܥܝܢ
40	ܐܪ̈ܒܥܝܢ	80	ܬܡܢܝܢ
50	ܚܡܫܝܢ	90	ܬܫܥܝܢ

These combine with the numbers 1-9, as in ܬܠܬܝܢ ܘܚܕܐ ܢܫ̈ܐ 'thirty-one women'.

Larger numbers are as follows:

ܡܐܐ 'one hundred'; ܬܪ̈ܬܡܐܐ 'two hundred'; but ܬܠܬܡܐܐ 'three hundred', ܐܪ̈ܒܥܡܐܐ '400', etc.

ܐܠܦ/ 'one thousand'. This is the absolute form, most usually seen. The plural is ܐܠܦ̈ܝܢ/, as in ܫܒܥ ܐܠܦ̈ܝܢ ܫܢܝܢ 'seven thousand years'.

ܪܒܘܬܐ 'ten thousand' (f.), also absolute; pl. ܪܒܘ̈ܢ.

Ordinal numbers ('first', 'second', etc.) exist from 1 to 10. They are as follows in the m. emph.:

1st	ܩܕܡܝܐ	6th	ܫܬܝܬܝܐ
2nd	ܬܪܝܢܐ (f. ܬܪܬܝܢܝܬܐ)	7th	ܫܒܝܥܝܐ
3rd	ܬܠܝܬܝܐ	8th	ܬܡܝܢܝܐ
4th	ܪܒܝܥܝܐ	9th	ܬܫܝܥܝܐ
5th	ܚܡܝܫܝܐ	10th	ܥܣܝܪܝܐ.

Alternatively, and for numbers above ten, the ordinal number is made by prefixing ܕ to the cardinal number, e.g. ܝܘܡܐ ܕܚܡܫܐ 'the fifth day'. For higher numbers, it is common to use the construct of the noun before the cardinal number, e.g. ܫܢܬ /ܐܪܒܥܡܐܐ ܘܥܣܪܝܢ ܘܚܕܐ 'the 421st year'.

The days of the week are: ܚܕ ܒܫܒܐ Sunday; ܬܪܝܢ ܒܫܒܐ Monday; ܬܠܬܐ ܒܫܒܐ/ Tuesday; ܐܪܒܥܐ ܒܫܒܐ/ Wednesday; ܚܡܫܐ ܒܫܒܐ Thursday. Often these are written as one word: ܚܡܫܒܫܒܐ etc. Friday is ܥܪܘܒܬܐ ('eve', i.e., of the sabbath) and Saturday is ܫܒܬܐ.

In writing, numbers are often expressed by letters of the alphabet. In this system[2]

1-10	=	/ to ܝ
20-90	=	ܟ to ܨ

---

[2] Laid out fully in reference grammars, e.g. Costaz, *Grammaire syriaque*, 226-7.

100-400	=	ܩ to ܬ
500-900	=	ܢ̈ to ܨ̈ ; or ܬܩ ܬܪ ܬܫ ܬܬ ܬܬܩ
1000	=	ܐ
2000	=	ܐܐ or ܒ .

Often a line is drawn over the number. Examples are: ܬܟܙ = 527; ܐܬ̈ܩ ܘܡܕ = 1544.

Vocabulary

ܐܣܰܪ	bind, *o*	ܟܢܰܫ	*pe.* (*o*), *pa.* gather
ܟܠܠ	*ethpa.* be crowned, martyred	ܩܒܠ	*aph.* confront
ܝܰܪܚܳܐ	month	ܡܰܫܪܺܝܬܳܐ	army (*f.*)
ܬܠܺܝܬܳܝܽܘܬܳܐ	Trinity (*f.*)	ܫܳܘܶܐ	equal
ܡܶܢܝܳܢܳܐ	number, numeration	ܐܰܝܟ	approximately
ܩܢܽܘܡܳܐ	person, *hypostasis*	ܢܽܘܢܳܐ	fish
ܚܙܺܝܪܳܢ	June[3]	ܟܝܳܢܳܐ	nature
ܢܺܝܩܺܝܰܐ	Nicaea	ܚܢܽܘܟ	Enoch

Exercises

Translate into English:

1. ܒܢܺܝܩܺܝܰܐ ܐܶܬܟܰܢܰܫܘ ܬܠܳܬܡܳܐܐ ܘܬܡܳܢܬܰܥܣܰܪ ܐܶܦܺܣܩܽܘܦܶܐ ܡܶܢ ܟܽܠܗ̇ ܥܳܠܡܳܐ ܦܰܠܓܶܗ.
2. ܫܰܐܶܠ ܠܗܽܘܢ ܢܽܘܚ: ܡܳܢܳܐ ܬܶܒܥܽܘܢ ܐܰܝܟ ܠܟܽܘܢ. ܐܶܡܰܪܘ ܠܶܗ ܚܰܒܪܶܐ ܘܰܩܒܶܠ ܢܽܘܢܳܐ.
3. ܐܶܡܰܪ ܚܢܽܘܟ ܠܒܢܰܘܗ̱ܝ ܕܢܶܬܟܰܢܫܽܘܢ ܐܰܝܟ ܡܶܢ ܚܰܡܫܳܐ ܒܝܰܪܚܳܐ. ܘܗܳܘܳܐ ܢܚܶܬ ܠܗܽܘܢ ܒܝܽܘܡܳܐ ܠܟܽܠܗܽܘܢ ܕܬܡܳܢܰܥܣܰܪ ܒܶܗ ܒܝܰܪܚܳܐ.

[3] For the other months see Appendix D, p. 147.

4. ܐܡ̈ܪܐ ܬܫܥܝܢ ܘܬܫܥ ܫܒܩ ܒܛܘܪܐ. ܘܠܚܕܐ ܬܫܥܝܢ ܠܘܬ ܠܡܪ̈ܥܝܬܐ
ܘܐܙܠ ܘܐܬܐ ܐܚܪܢܐ ܠܡܪ̈ܥܝܬܐ ܘܬܫܥ.

5. ܗܪܘܕܣ ܡܠܟܐ ܩܛܠ ܛܠܝ̈ܐ ܟܠܗܘܢ ܕܒܝܬ ܠܚܡ ܡܢ ܒܪ ܬܪ̈ܬܝܢ
ܫܢܝ̈ܢ ܘܠܬܚܬ.

7. ܟܠܗܘܢ ܫܢ̈ܘܗܝ ܕܡܬܘܫܠܚ ܒܣܘܟܐ ܗܘ ܐܝܬܝܗܘܢ ܒܡܢܝܢܐ ܐܝܟ ܡܐܐ
ܘܐܪܒܥܝܢ.

8. ܡܬܘܡܝܢ ܐܢܐ ܠܟܡ ܒܡܠܟܘܬܐ ܩܕܝܫܬܐ: ܗܘܝܘ ܕܝܢ ܒܢܝ ܐܠܗܐ ܐܚܐ
ܒܪܐ ܘܙܘܥܐ ܕܫܘܪܐ: ܠܟܠܐ ܡܢܘܬܐ ܒܥܬܐ: ܕܟܢܝܐ ܡܢ ܐܢܘܢ:
ܒܡܢܘܬܐ ܕܝܢ ܠܟܠܐ.

9. ܘܫܘܪܐ ܕܡܕܝܢܬܐ ܐܝܬ ܠܗ ܬܪ̈ܥܐ ܬܪܬܥܣܪ. ܘܥܠܝܗܘܢ ܬܪܥܣܪ
ܫܡ̈ܗܐ ܕܫܠܝܚܘܗܝ ܕܒܪܐ.

10. ܒܐܪܒܥܐ ܘܬܡܢܝܢ ܒܢܝܣܢ ܕܫܢܬ ܫܬܡܐܐ ܘܫܒܥܝܢ ܘܐܪܒܥ ܒܡܠܟܘܬܐ
ܕܝܘܢܝ̈ܐ: ܒܗ ܒܝܘܡܐ ܗܢܐ ܐܬܚܙܝ ܗܘܐ ܟܘܟܒܐ ܚܕܐ ܠܚܕܐ.

Translate into Syriac:

1. 3,428 men. 2. There are two ways from which one shall choose; one is good and the other is bad. 3. On the fifteenth day of the month the city fell. 4. The three of them went into the house. 5. The number of the elect (*lit.* chosen) was 144,000. 6. All the days of Adam were 930 years. 7. Enoch was the seventh from Adam. 8. The apostles took 153 fish from the sea. 9. He chose twelve that they should be with him. 10. Moses appointed seventy-two elders that they should judge the people.

APPENDIX A
PRONUNCIATION OF THE BGDKPT LETTERS

The rule given on p. 11 takes care of most circumstances: a
bgdkpt letter is pronounced hard (that is, with *qushaya*) after
a consonant, and soft (with *rukaka*) after a vowel. The most
important exceptions and special cases are covered by the
following rules. These rules are not always precise, however, and sometimes the authorities differ.

1. When a *bgdkpt* letter is doubled, it is pronounced hard.
Doubling is not shown in the script; it belongs to the underlying form of a word. The second radical letter is doubled
in forms of the pa'el and ethpa'al, e.g. ܩܒܠ *qabbel,* and in
nouns derived from these conjugations, e.g. ܡܐܟܠܐ, ܡܣܚܠܢܐ,
etc. Geminate roots give rise to many words with doubled
letters, e.g. ܐܟܠ, ܟܟܠ; likewise *pe-nun* verbs, in forms where
the *nun* changes to a doubled second root letter, as in ܐܦܩ,
ܡܦܩܬܐ ('a fall'). Verb forms beginning with *alaph*, especially the 1st sing. impf. pa'el, sometimes double the next
letter, e.g. ܐܘܒܟ 'I shall sacrifice'.

2. A *bgdkpt* letter following a diphthong (*ay, aw*) is pronounced hard, as in ܟܝܐ, ܡܘܬܐ .

3. A *bgdkpt* letter following an indistinct vowel (*shewa*) is
pronounced soft. These indistinct vowels are not shown in
the script. Sometimes it is easy to see that they are present,
as in ܟܬܒ *k'tab,* ܕܚܠܬܐ *dehl'tā,* and after a doubled letter, as
in ܐܬܠܒܒܬ *etlabb'bet* 'I was encouraged' or ܡܠܠܬܐ *mell'tā*

(from ܡܠܟ). In other cases, they cannot be detected except by reference to etymology, the *shewa* being the remnant of a full vowel in an older form of the word. Sometimes it is not clear whether even a *shewa* remains, but *rukaka* still applies. Examples are ܕܗܒܐ 'gold', ܚܡܬܐ 'anger', ܐܠܦܐ 'boat'. Such words have to be remembered when they are met. See also 7. below.

4. Words having a *shewa* after the first letter, like ܟܬܒ or ܩܕܡ, keep it when one of the inseparable prefixes is attached. This means that if the second letter is a *bgdkpt*, it remains soft: thus ܕܟܬܒ and ܘܩܕܡ .

5. The ܬ of the 2nd person perfect of the verb is hard even after a vowel, as in ܫܬܩܬ, ܫܬܩܬܝ, ܫܬܩܬܘܢ, ܫܬܩܬܝܢ 'you were silent'. The ܬ of the 3rd feminine is soft even when there is no vowel before it, as in ܩܛܠܬܗ 'she killed him'. The suffixes -ܟܘܢ and -ܟܝܢ are pronounced soft, but hard after the *ay* of the 'plural' forms; thus ܕܡܠܟܘܢ but ܕܡܠܟܝܟܘܢ .

6. The ܬ of feminine nouns is sometimes pronounced with *rukaka* after a consonant (that is, against the general rule). This happens most often when the preceding syllable has a short *a* or *e* vowel, as in ܩܛܠܬܐ (and other f. emph. ptcs.), ܕܡܟܬܐ, ܫܢܬܐ 'sleep'; or after ܥ, as in ܫܥܬܐ 'hour'. But there are many exceptions, e.g. ܐܓܪܬܐ, ܬܫܡܫܬܐ 'service'; and some words are attested both ways, e.g. ܡܘܗܒܬܐ / ܡܘܗܒܬܐ.

7. Some pairs of homographs are more or less artificially distinguished by *qushaya* and *rukaka*, including: ܩܫܬܐ 'bow'/ ܩܫܬܐ 'stubble'; ܓܪܒܐ 'leprosy'/ ܓܪܒܐ 'leper'; ܚܣܕܐ 'mercy'/ ܚܣܕܐ 'shame'.

APPENDIX B
THE ESTRANGELA SCRIPT. DIACRITICAL POINTS

The estrangela script is the earliest form of Syriac writing, being found in all manuscripts before the seventh century, and in many later ones. It is the script in which most scholarly editions are now printed. The following are the usual printed forms of the letters:

ܐ ܒ ܓ ܕ ܗ ܘ ܙ ܚ ܛ ܝ ܟ ܠ ܡ ܢ ܣ ܥ ܦ ܨ ܩ ܪ ܫ ܬ

These are the stand-alone forms, except for the letters that have final forms: *kaph*: ܟ ܟ *mem* : ܡ ܡ *nun*: ܢ ܢ . Final *shin* may also be cropped on the left: ܫ . The letters connect in the same way as their serto counterparts, except for *teth* which connects only at the base-line (i.e., ܛܒ) and *semkath* which, at least in early manuscripts, does not connect to a following letter (so that we find e.g. ܣܘܡ not ܣܘܡ). There is no contracted form of ܐܠ. The estrangela script generally presents no special problems to the West Syriac reader, except that it is usually printed without vowel-signs.

Diacritical points. Various kinds of points are found in an unvocalized text to help the reader distinguish among possible readings from a particular spelling. Of these, *seyame* (plural points) and the point on the feminine suffix ܗ-[1] are familiar from their use throughout this book. Of the other

---

[1] The estrangela script will be used for examples here, but these points are found with all three scripts even alongside vowel-signs.

kinds of diacritical points the following are the most often encountered.

1. *Pronouns.* A point *above* certain pronouns indicates the demonstrative; *below*, the personal. Thus:

ܗܘ = ܗܘ̇	that		ܗܝ = ܗܝ̇	that
ܗܘ = ܗ̇ܘ	he, it		ܗܝ = ܗ̇ܝ	she, it
ܗܢܘܢ = ܗܢܘ̇ܢ	those (*m.*)		ܗܢܝܢ = ܗܢܝ̇ܢ	those (*f.*)
ܗܢܘܢ = ܗ̇ܢܘܢ	they (*m.*)		ܗܢܝܢ = ܗ̇ܢܝܢ	they (*f.*).

2. *Verbs.* There are several uses of the diacritical point.

a. A point *above* a three-letter verb indicates the participle; *below*, the perfect. For example,

$$\text{ܦܩܕ} = \text{ܦ̇ܩܕ} \quad \text{commanding}$$
$$\text{ܦܩܕ} = \text{ܦܩ̣ܕ} \quad \text{commanded.}$$

In *lamad-yod* verbs, the passive participle also looks the same, and may be distinguished by a point *below*. Thus ܓܒܐ might be ܓ̇ܒܐ 'chosen' or ܓܒ̣ܐ 'chose'.

b. A point *above* a verb form can indicate the pa'el; *below*, the pe'al, as in:

$$\text{ܩܪܒ} = \text{ܩܪ̇ܒ} \quad \text{offered}$$
$$\text{ܩܪܒ} = \text{ܩܪ̣ܒ} \quad \text{approached.}$$

c. In forms of the pa'el and aph'el that have a preformative, a point *above*, over the syllable with the vowel, distinguishes one from the other, as in:

$$\text{ܡܩܒܠ} = \text{ܡܩܒ̇ܠ} \quad \text{receiving}$$
$$\text{ܡܩܒܠ} = \text{ܡ̇ܩܒܠ} \quad \text{confronting.}$$

d. Points distinguish the 1st, 2nd masculine and 3rd feminine singular perfect of the verb, which would otherwise
   look identical, as follows:

$$\text{ܩܶܛܠܶܬ} = \text{ܩܛܠܬ}\quad \text{I killed}$$
$$\text{ܩܛܰܠܬ} = \text{ܩܛܠܬ}\quad \text{you (}m\text{.) killed}$$
$$\text{ܩܶܛܠܰܬ} = \text{ܩܛܠܬ}\quad \text{she killed.}$$

3. *Other homographs.* Points distinguish many common
pairs of words. A general rule is that a point *above* indicates
the word with the fuller stronger vocalization; *below*, the
weaker one. But some points are arbitrary. Examples are:

ܥܒܳܕܐ = deed		ܐܝܕܳܐ = which (f.)	
ܥܰܒܕܐ = servant		ܐܝܕܐ = hand	
ܡܰܢ = who		ܡܰܢܘ = who?	
ܡܶܢ = from		ܡܳܢܘ = what?	
ܡܰܠܟܐ = king		ܫܰܢܬܐ = year	
ܡܶܠܟܐ = counsel		ܫܶܢܬܐ = sleep	

$$\text{ܥܰܘܳܠ}\quad \text{iniquitous one}$$
$$\text{ܥܰܘܠܐ}\quad \text{iniquity (or ܥܽܘܠܐ baby).}$$

Exercise. Read the following (Psalm 1: 1-3).

[Syriac text of Psalm 1:1-3]

144

APPENDIX C
EAST SYRIAC WRITING AND PHONOLOGY

Mesopotamia & points East

To read an East Syriac text it is not necessary to learn any grammar different from that covered in this book. The unfamiliar features are in the writing system and in some relatively small matters of phonology.

The script. The following are the forms of the letters:

ܐ ܒ ܓ ܕ ܗ ܘ ܙ ܚ ܛ ܝ ܟ ܠ ܡ ܢ ܣ ܥ ܦ ܨ ܩ ܪ ܫ ܬ

These are the stand-alone forms, except for *kaph*, *mem*, and *nun* which, as in the other scripts, have different final forms: for *kaph* ܟ or ܒ ; for *mem* ܡ ; for *nun* ܢ or ܢ . (As in the estrangela script, *lamad* and *'e* have no different final forms, and there is no ligature for *lamad-alaph*.) A contracted form of *tau-alaph* ܠ is often used when the *tau* is connected to a previous letter, as in ܬܐ (W. Syriac ܬܐ). Another ligatured form ܬ also sometimes appears.

The letters most likely to be confusing to a West Syriac reader are the following.

ܐ (*alaph*) has a base-line stroke and accidentally resembles serto *tau* (ܠ). The East Syriac *tau* ܬ always has a beginning up-stroke, even when not connected from the right.

ܕ ܪ (*dalath* and *resh*) have nearly the same shape as ܟ (*kaph*). Their large square dots should distinguish them, but notice also that *dalath* and *resh* do not connect on the left.

ܘ (*zayn*) looks somewhat like serto ܘ or ܙ, but it has no dot.

ܟ (final *kaph* connected from the right) has to be distinguished from ܢ (final *nun*).

Vowels and vowel-signs. East Syriac distinguishes *seven* vowels, indicated by dots.[1] (When correctly written or printed, these are short oblique lines and less bold than the diacritical points.) The correspondence with the system of vowels used in this book is as follows:

scriptis plena (matres lectionis)
whether long or short

ܵ	*bā*	=	ܿ	ܸܝ	*bi*	=	ܝ
ܲ	*ba*	=	ܲ	ܘ	*bo*	=	ܘ [2]
ܹ	*be*	=	ܹ	ܘ	*bu*	=	ܘ
ܹ	*bē*	=	ܹ or ܹ				

Examples of words that have the vowel *ē* in the East Syriac system and *i* in the West, are: ܡܕܡܕܐ (ܡܟܪܡܙܐ) and other words where the vowel is carried by *alaph*; the 1st sing. of *lamad-yod* verbs, e.g. ܟܬܒܬ (ܟܬܒܬ); and the preformatives on *pe-alaph* verbs like ܢܐܡܪ (ܢܐܡܪ).

Other signs in writing. East Syriac texts are typically written or printed with vowels, *qushaya* and *rukaka*, and diacritical points. (The result can be a swarm of dots that have to be distinguished.)

There are a few diacritical points different from those described in Appendix B above, chiefly the following:

ܡܗܠܟ = ܡܗܠܟ (3rd. f. sing. pf.)

ܘܗܝ = ܘܗܝ ܒܗ = ܒܗ ܘܗܘ = ܘܗܘ (all non-enclitic forms).

---

[1] Sometimes these vowels are seen in West Syriac manuscripts too.

[2] Recall (p. 13 above) that in a pure West Syriac text this vowel is not distinguished from ܘ.

Linea occultans is written above, not below, a letter; e.g.,
ܡܕܝܼܢ̈ܬܐ. An oblique line below a letter can indicate a short
vowel introduced into a cluster of consonants, e.g. ܕܹܚܠܬܐ
(*dehelṭa*). A small *alaph* is often written above initial *yod*, as
in ܝܼܕܥ (for ܝܺܕܰܥ). *renders pronunciation* اَلتُّرْكُ

Pronunciation. The following are the chief differences to be
observed in the East Syriac system.

1. *Alaph* does not quiesce after a preceding vowelless letter,
e.g. ܥܒܕ (not ܥܒܕ; cf. W. Syr. ܚ̈ܠܐ), ܘܐܕܝܼܢ (W. Syr. ܘܐܦܠܐ).

NB →

2. Instead of the W. Syriac diphthong *aw*, E. Syriac usually
has *āw*, e.g. ܗܘ݂ܐ (for ܗܘܐ), ܢܗܘܒ (for ܢܗܘܒ).

3. The letter ܟ is rarely spirantized, and is not marked with
qushaya or *rukaka*. In the few words where it is pronounced
soft, like ܢܘܟܬ, it may have a semicircular mark under it.

4. The name Jesus is ܝܫܘܥ or ܝܼܫܘܥ (hence *Išoʿ* not *Yešuʿ*).

Exercise. Read the following (the Lord's Prayer; cf. §28
exercise no. 10).

ܐܒܘܢ ܕܒܫܡܝܐ ܢܬܩܕܫ ܫܡܟ. ܬܐܬܐ ܡܠܟܘܬܟ. ܢܗܘܐ ܨܒܝܢܟ. ܐܝܟܢܐ
ܕܒܫܡܝܐ ܐܦ ܒܐܪܥܐ. ܗܒ ܠܢ ܠܚܡܐ ܕܣܘܢܩܢܢ ܝܘܡܢܐ. ܘܫܒܘܩ ܠܢ
ܚܘܒܝܢ. ܐܝܟܢܐ ܕܐܦ ܚܢܢ ܫܒܩܢ ܠܚܝܒܝܢ. ܘܠܐ ܬܥܠܢ ܠܢܣܝܘܢܐ.
ܐܠܐ ܦܨܢ ܡܢ ܒܝܫܐ. ܡܛܠ ܕܕܝܠܟ ܗܝ ܡܠܟܘܬܐ ܘܚܝܠܐ
ܘܬܫܒܘܚܬܐ ܠܥܠܡ ܥܠܡܝܢ. ܐܡܝܢ.

Jesus in Koran = ʿĪsā – *a calque on E Syriac* Išoʿ
ܝܫܘܥ

APPENDIX D
DATES

Syriac sources use the Julian calendar but the names for the months are indigenous. These are as follows:

October	ܬܫܪܝܢ ܩܕܝܡ	Teshri I
November	ܬܫܪܝܢ ܐܚܪܝܢ	Teshri II
December	ܟܢܘܢ ܩܕܝܡ	Kanun I
January	ܟܢܘܢ ܐܚܪܝܢ	Kanun II
February	ܫܒܛ	Shebaṭ
March	ܐܕܪ	Adar
April	ܢܝܣܢ	Nisan
May	ܐܝܪ	Iyar
June	ܚܙܝܪܢ	Ḥaziran
July	ܬܡܘܙ	Tammuz
August	ܐܒ	Ab
September	ܐܝܠܘܠ	Elul.

There are some variants: ܬܫܪܝ for ܬܫܪܝܢ; ܩܕܡ for ܩܕܝܡ; ܐܚܪܝܐ for ܐܚܪܝܢ. A later name for August is ܛܒܚ.

Dates are given, even in some modern sources, according to the Seleucid era (usually styled ܕܝܘܢܝܐ, 'of the Greeks'), reckoned to have begun on the first day of October (Teshri I), 312 BCE. To convert a date of this kind to a date CE, subtract 311, or 312 if the month is Teshri I or II or Kanun I. Thus, the date in §29 exercise no. 4

ܐܪܒܥܐ ܘܥܣܪܝܢ ܒܚܙܝܪܢ ܕܫܢܬ ܫܬܡܐܐ ܘܫܒܥܝܢ ܘܐܪܒܥ ܒܡܢܝܢܐ ܕܝܘܢܝܐ

is 24 June 674 of the Seleucid era or 24 June 363 CE.

Two manuscript colophons will serve as further examples of Syriac dates and their conversion.

ܐܫܬܠܡܬ ܦܢܩܝܬܐ ܗܕܐ ܒܝܪܚ ܬܫܪܝ ܐܚܪܝ ܫܢܬ
ܫܒܥܡܐܐ ܘܥܣܪܝܢ ܘܬܠܬ ܒܐܘܪܗܝ ܡܕܝܢܬܐ ܕܒܝܬ
ܢܗܪܝܢ.

> This volume was completed in the month Teshri II in the year seven hundred and twenty-three at Edessa, a city of Mesopotamia.

Since the month is Teshri II (November), the calculation is

723 − 312 = 411 CE.[1]

The same calculation may be applied to this modern manuscript colophon:[2]

ܫܠܡ ܒܥܘܕܪܢ ܡܪܢ ܘܐܠܗܢ ܟܬܒܐ ܗܢܐ ܕܫܥܝ̈ܬܐ ܒܝܪܚܐ ܒܪܝܟܐ
ܬܫܪܝܢ ܐܚܪܝܢ ܒܚܡܫܒܫܒܐ ܝ̇ܕ ܒܗ ܒܫܢܬ ܒ//ܩܡܙ ܠܝܘܢܝ̈ܐ
ܒܪܝ̈ܟܐ.

> This book of stories was finished, by the help of our Lord and God, in the blessed month Teshri II, on Thursday the fourteenth [day] in it, in the year 2147 of the blessed Greeks.

This date works out to be 14 November 1835.[3]

[1] MS British Library Add. 12150, the earliest surviving Syriac manuscript that is dated.

[2] MS Selly Oak Colleges Library Mingana Syr. 502.

[3] Or 25 November 1835 in the Western (Gregorian) calendar.

SYRIAC - ENGLISH GLOSSARY

In this glossary, nouns are quoted in the emphatic state, adjectives in the masculine absolute. Verbs are quoted in the pe‘al perefect when this is actually used (except for hollow verbs where the full root is given). This form shows the correct stem vowel (ˊ or ˋ) in the perfect. The English letter a, e, or o following indicates the vowel of the imperfect. Verbs not used in the pe‘al are quoted without vowels on the root letters. References to the grammar indicate that more details about inflection or usage may be found there.

ܐ *ālap*

ܐܒ August

ܐܒܐ father; §12

ܐܒܕ perish, be lost, a; aph. destroy, lose; §21

ܐܒܠ pass. ptc. ܐܒܝܠ mourning; ethp. mourn; §21

ܐܒܪܗܡ Abraham

ܐܕܡ Adam

ܐܓܪܐ roof

ܐܓܪܐ wages

ܐܓܪܬܐ letter

ܐܕܪ March

ܐܘ or

ܐܘ o (vocative)

ܐܘܢܓܠܝܘܢ gospel

ܐܘܪܚܐ road, way (f.); pl. ܐܘܪ̈ܚܬܐ

ܐܘܪܗܝ Edessa

ܐܘܪܫܠܡ Jerusalem

ܐܙܠ go, a; §21

ܐܚܐ brother; §12

ܐܚܕ hold, seize, close, o; §21

ܐܚܪ aph. delay; §21

ܐܚܪܝ last, latter; §12

ܐܚܪܢ other, another; §12

اِیدَا hand (f.), cstr. اِید ; حمل
by means of; §12

اِیدَا (f. of اَیلَ) which, who

اِیزَخَا emissary

اَیِک like, as, approximately

اَیکَا where

اَیکَنَا how, as, in order that

اَیلِین (pl.) which, who; §4

اِیلَانَا tree

اِیمَمَا daytime

اَینَا which, who (m.)

اِسرَاییِل Israel

اِیقَارَا honour

اِیَر May

اِیت there is, there are; §7

اِیتَوهِ- like (+ suffixes); §7

اَخَل eat, consume, o; §21.
اَخَل قَرصَا accuse,
slander

اَخِلقَرصَا Satan

اَخسَنَیَا stranger

اِلَا but; unless

اَلَاهَا God

اِلُّو if (contrary to fact)

اِیلُول September

اَلَف one thousand; §29

اَلِف teach; §21

اَلَص pe. (o), pa. press,
compel, oppress; §21

اِمَا mother; §12

اَمِین amen

اِمَر say, a; §21

اِمرَا lamb; §11

اِمَتَی when?, sometimes

اِمَتَی وِ- when

اِن if

اِنَا / اِن، نَا I

اِنَّون (enclitic form of هِنُّون)
they (m.)

اِنِّین (enclitic form of هِنِّین)
they (f.)

اِنَاش someone, one; لَا اِنَاش
no one; کُل اِنَاش
everyone; §12

اِنَاشَا people (pl.); §12

اِنَاشَی (adj.) human

اَنت you (m.)

اَنتُون you (m. pl.)

اَنتِی you (f.)

اَنتِّین you (f. pl.)

ܐܰܢ̱ܬܬܳܐ/ woman, wife (*f.*); *pl.*
ܢܶܫ̈ܐ; §12

ܐܶܣܛܪܰܛܝܽܘܛܐ/ soldier

ܐܶܣܦܪܺܝܕܐ/ basket

ܐܶܣܰܪ/ bind, *o*; §21

ܐܳܦ/ also, even

ܐܶܦܺܣܩܳܘܦܐ/ bishop

ܐܰܦܪܶܡ/ Ephrem

ܐܰܪܒܥܐ/ four; §29

ܐܰܪܡܰܠܬܐ/ widow (*f.*)

ܐܰܪܥܐ/ land (*f.*); *pl.* ܐܰܪ̈ܥܬܐ/

ܐܶܫܟܰܚ/ find, be able; §17

ܐܶܫܰܕ/ pour out, *o*; §21

ܐܶܬܐ/ come; *aph.* bring; §27

ܐܰܬܪܐ/ place (*m.*); *pl.* ܐܰܬܪ̈ܰܘܳܬܐ/

ܒ *bet*

ܒ- in, by, with; §7

ܒܶܐܫ be bad, *a*; *aph.* do
evil; §23

ܒܳܒܶܠ Babylon

ܒܗܶܬ be ashamed, *a*

ܒܽܘܪܟܬܐ blessing (*f.*)

ܒܰܙ plunder, *o*; §25

ܒܶܝܬ or ܒܶܝܢ between,
among; §7

ܒܺܝܪܬܐ fortress, palace (*f.*)

ܒܺܝܫ evil

ܒܰܝܢ (*prep.*) between,
among (= ܒܶܝܬ)

ܒܶܝܬ ܐܰܣܺܝܪ̈ܐ (in) prison

ܒܶܝܬ ܢܰܗܪ̈ܝܢ Mesopotamia

ܒܰܝܬܐ house; §12

ܒܰܠܒܶܠ *palpel* confuse; §25

ܒܰܠܚܽܘܕ alone; §11

ܒܶܠܥܳܕ without; §11

ܒܢܐ build

ܒܶܣܪܐ flesh, meat

ܒܥܐ ask for, seek, require;
§26

ܒܳܥܽܘܬܐ petition (*f.*)

ܒܥܶܠܕܒܳܒܐ enemy

ܒܰܪ *cstr. of* ܒܪܐ; *see also* ܠܒܰܪ

ܒܰܪܢܳܫܐ or ܒܰܪ ܐ̱ܢܳܫܐ/ person; §12

ܒܪܐ son; §12

ܒܪܐ create; §27

ܒܳܪܽܘܝܐ creator

ܒܪܺܝܟ blessed

ܒܰܪܶܟ *pa.* bless

ܒܪܫܝܬ in the beginning; Genesis

ܒܪܬܐ daughter; §12

ܒܬܪ after; §11

gāmal

ܓܒܐ choose; §26

ܓܒܠ form, fashion, o

ܓܒܪܐ man

ܓܕܦ pa. blaspheme

ܓܘܐ (n.) inside; cstr. ܓܘ

ܓܘܕܦܐ blasphemy

ܓܘܫܡܐ body

ܓܝܪ (conj.) for, however (like Greek γάρ)

ܓܠܐ reveal, make clear

ܓܢܬܐ garden (f.)

ܓܪܡܐ bone

ܓܫܡ touch, o; §25

dālat

ܕ- of, which, who; §7

ܕܒܚ pa. sacrifice

ܕܒܚܬܐ sacrifice (f.)

ܕܒܪ lead, a; pa. govern

ܕܗܒܐ gold

ܕܘܝ act. part. ܕܘܝ wretched

ܕܘܝܕ David

ܕܘܒܪܐ way of life (pl.)

ܕܘܟܐ (m.) or ܕܘܟܬܐ (f.); pl. ܕܘܟܬܐ place

ܕܘܢ judge; §24

ܕܚܠ fear, be afraid (+ܡܢ of), a

ܕܚܠܬܐ fear (f.)

ܕܝܠ- of, belonging to; §7

ܕܝܢ (conj.) but, however (like Greek δέ)

ܕܝܢܐ judgement

ܕܝܢܐ judge

ܕܝܪܐ monastery (f.); pl. ܕܝܪܬܐ

ܕܝܪܝܐ monk

ܕܝܬܩܐ testament (f.)

ܕܟܐ or ܕܟܐ be pure; pa. purify; §28

ܕܠܐ without

ܕܠܡܐ lest, perhaps

ܕܡܐ blood; abs., cstr. ܕܡ

ܕܡܐ be like; pa. liken; §27

ܕܡܥܬܐ tear (of the eye; f.); pl. ܕܡܥܐ

ܗܘ *he*

ܗܐ behold

ܗܕܐ (*f.* of ܗܢܐ) this

ܗܓܐ *ethpa.* meditate

ܗܓܡܘܢܐ governor

ܗܘ he; *enclitic* ܗܘ; §4

ܗܘ that (*m.*); §4

ܗܘܐ be, become; §26

ܗܘܐ (*enclitic*) was; §14

ܗܘܝܘ it is (*m.*)

ܗܝ she; *enclitic* ܗܝ; §4

ܗܝ that (*f.*); §4

ܗܝ ܕ- the fact that

ܗܝܕܝܢ then

ܗܝܟܠܐ temple, palace

ܗܝܡܢ believe; §16

ܗܝܡܢܘܬܐ faith (*f.*)

ܗܟܢܐ thus, so

ܗܠܟ *pa.* walk

ܗܢܐ this (*m.*); §4

ܗܢܘܢ they (*m.*); §4

ܗܢܘܢ those (*m.*); §4

ܗܢܝܢ they (*f.*); §4

ܗܢܝܢ those (*f.*); §4

ܗܦܟ return, go back, *o*

ܗܪܛܝܩܐ heretic

ܗܪܟܐ here

ܗܫܐ now

ܘ *waw*

ܘ- and; §4

ܘܝ woe

ܘܠܐ *act. ptcs.* ܘܠܐ, ܡܘܠܐ be fitting; §14

ܙ *zayn*

ܙܒܢ buy, *e*; *pa.* sell

ܙܒܢܐ time; *abs., cstr.* ܙܒܢ

ܙܕܩ *act. ptc.* ܙܕܩ be right; *pa.* justify

ܙܕܝܩܘܬܐ righteousness (*f.*)

ܙܗܪ *pa.* warn; *ethp.* take care (+-ܒ) of, guard

ܙܘܙܐ coin

ܙܘܥ shake, move (*intrans.*); *aph.* set in motion; §24

ܙܘܥܐ movement, quake

ܙܡܪ *pe.* (*a*), *pa.* sing

ܙܢܐ kind, type; §12

ܙܥܘܪ small; *f.* ܙܥܘܪܬܐ

ܙܰܪܥܳܐ seed

ܚܶܝܬ *ḥeṯ*

ܚܒ *aph.* love; §25

ܚܰܒܺܝܒ beloved

ܚܰܒܪܳܐ companion; *f.* ܚܰܒܪܬܳܐ

ܚܰܕ one, a; *f.* ܚܕܳܐ

ܚܰܕܽܘܬܳܐ rejoicing (*f.*)

ܚܕܺܝ or ܚܕܳܐ rejoice; §26

ܚܕܰܬ new; *emph.* ܚܰܕܬܳܐ;
f. emph. ܚܕܰܬܳܐ

ܚܘܳܐ *pa.* show; §27

ܚܰܘܳܐ Eve

ܚܳܒ owe, be wrong; *pa.* convict

ܚܽܘܒܳܐ love

ܚܰܘܒܳܐ debt, sin

ܚܽܘܪ look (+ ܒ- at)

ܚܰܘܳܪ white

ܚܙܳܐ see; §26; *ethp.* appear

ܚܶܙܘܳܐ vision, appearance

ܚܙܺܝܪܳܢ June; §29

ܚܰܛܳܝܳܐ sinner

ܚܛܳܗܳܐ sin

ܚܛܺܝܬܳܐ sin (*f.*; *abstract*)

ܚܰܝ living

ܚܝܳܐ live; *aph.* save; §27

ܚܰܝ̈ܶܐ life, salvation (*pl.*)

ܚܰܝܳܒ indebted, guilty

ܚܰܝܘܬܳܐ animal(s) (*f. sing.*)

ܚܝܠ *pa.* strengthen

ܚܰܝܠܳܐ strength, force,
mighty work

ܚܰܟܺܝܡ wise

ܚܶܟܡܬܳܐ wisdom (*f.*)

ܚܠܺܝܡ *pe. pass. ptc.* well,
whole; *ethp.* be made
well

ܚܠܦ *shaph.* change

ܚܠܳܦ for, instead of; §11

ܚܶܠܩܳܐ fate

ܚܡܳܪܳܐ (male) donkey

ܚܰܡܶܫ five; §29

ܚܰܢ show mercy to, *o*; §25

ܚܢܰܓܬܳܐ groan; *pl.* ܚ̈ܢܳܓܳܬܳܐ

ܚܢܰܢ, ܚܢܰܢ we; §4

ܚܳܣ far be it!

ܚܰܣܺܝܢ strong

ܚܶܪܝܳܢܳܐ dispute, contention

ܚܰܩܠܳܐ field (*f.*)

ܣܡ suffer, a; §25

ܣܡܟ reckon, o

ܐܚܬܐ sister (f.); §12

ٮ teṯ

ܛܐܒ be good; aph. do
good; §23

ܛܒܐ or ܛܒܟܐ news

ܛܒ (adj.) good; (adv.)
very, very much

ܛܒܬܐ good; §28

ܛܘܒ happy are (+sfx.+ -ܠ)

ܛܘܒܢܐ blessed one (m.);
ܛܘܒܢܬܐ (f.)

ܛܘܪܐ mountain

ܛܝܒܘܬܐ grace, favour (f.)

ܛܝܡܐ price (pl.)

ܛܠܝܐ child; pl. usu. ܛܠܝܐ;
f. ܛܠܝܬܐ, f. pl. ܛܠܝܬܐ

ܛܠܝܘܬܐ childhood (f.)

ܛܥܡ taste, a

ܛܪܦܐ leaf

ܝ yoḏ

ܝܒܠ aph. bring, carry; pa.
transmit; §22

ܝܕܐ aph. confess, thank; §27

ܝܕܥ know; §22; aph.
inform, make known

ܝܗܒ give; §22

ܝܗܘܕܝܐ Jew

ܝܗܘܕܐ Judas

ܝܘܚܢܢ John

ܝܘܠܦܢܐ doctrine

ܝܘܡܐ day (m.); abs., cstr.
ܝܘܡ ; pl. usu. ܝܘܡܬܐ

ܝܘܡܢܐ today

ܝܘܢ (adj.) Greek

ܝܠܕ give birth to, a; ethp.
be born; aph. beget;
§22

ܝܠܠ aph. ܐܝܠܠ wail

ܝܠܦ learn, a; §22

ܝܡܐ sea

ܝܡܝܢܐ right, right hand (f.)

ܝܢܩ aph. ܐܝܢܩ suckle; §22

ܝܥܩܘܒ Jacob, James

ܝܨܦ be anxious, take care,
a; §22

ܝܩܕ burn, a (intransitive);
aph. burn (trans.); §22

ܝܺܩܰܪ be heavy, *a*; *pa.* honour; §22

ܝܰܪܚܳܐ month

ܝܺܪܶܬ inherit, *a*; §22

ܝܶܫܽܘܥ Jesus, Joshua

ܝܰܫܶܛ *aph.* stretch out; §22

ܝܺܬܶܒ sit, dwell; §22

ܝܺܬܰܪ gain, abound, remain over; §22

ܝܰܬܺܝܪ more (+ ܡܶܢ than)

ܝܰܬܺܝܪܳܐܝܺܬ especially

ܟ ¹ *kap*

ܟܺܐܢ just, righteous

ܟܺܐܢܳܐܝܺܬ justly

ܟܺܐܢܽܘܬܳܐ justice

ܟܺܐܦܳܐ stone (*f.*)

ܟܰܕ when, while; §10

ܟܳܗܢܳܐ priest

ܟܝܳܢܳܐ nature

ܟܽܠ all, every; §7

ܟܠܠ *ethpa.* be crowned, be martyred

---

¹ This is the usual way of writing the letter *kaph* alone. Cf. *nun* (ܢ) and *mem* (ܡܡ).

ܟܠܺܝܠܳܐ crown

ܟܠܡܶܕܶܡ everything

ܟܽܠܡܰܢ ܕ- whoever

ܟܠܢܳܫ everyone

ܟܡܳܐ how much, how many

ܟܶܢ next

ܟܳܢܽܘܢ ܐ̱ܚܪܳܝ January

ܟܳܢܽܘܢ ܩܰܕܡܳܝ December

ܟܢܽܘܫܬܳܐ synagogue (*f.*)

ܟܢܰܫ gather, *o*

ܟܶܢܫܳܐ crowd

ܟܣܣ *aph.* reprove; *ethp.* be reproved; §25

ܟܣܺܝ *pe., pa.* hide, cover; §28

ܟܪܶܗ *ethp.* be ill; *pe. pass. ptc.* ܟܪܺܝܗ ill, sick

ܟܪܰܙ *aph.* preach; *ethp.* be preached

ܟܪܺܣܛܝܳܢܳܐ (*adj.*) Christian

ܟܪܰܟ *ethp.* go around

ܟܰܪܡܳܐ vineyard

ܟܰܪܣܳܐ womb (*f.*)

ܟܬܰܒ write, *o*

ܟܬܳܒܳܐ book, Scripture

ܠ *lāmad*

ܠ to, for; *sign of a definite direct object*; §8

ܠܐ not, no. ܘܠܐ without

ܠܒܐ heart

ܠܒܒ *pa.* encourage

ܠܒܘܫܐ clothing, garment

ܠܒܫ be dressed, *a*; *aph.* clothe

ܠܒܪ (ܡܢ) outside; §11

ܠܓܘ (ܡܢ) inside; §11

ܠܟ (= ܠܐ ܗܘ) not

ܠܘܐ *pa.* accompany; §28

ܠܘܛ curse; §24

ܠܘܩܒܠ against; §11

ܠܘܩܕܡ (*adv.*) first, beforehand

ܠܘܬ toward, around; §7

ܠܚܡܐ bread

ܠܝܬ (= ܠܐ ܐܝܬ) there is not

ܠܠܝܐ night (*f.*)

ܠܡ *particle indicating direct speech*

ܠܡܢܐ why

ܠܣܛܝܐ robber

ܠܥܠ (ܡܢ) above; §11

ܠܫܢܐ language

ܠܬܚܬ (ܡܢ) below; §11

ܡܝܡ *mem*

ܡܐ what

ܡܐ ܕ when

ܡܐܐ one hundred; §29

ܡܐܟܘܠܬܐ food (*f.*); *pl.* ܡܐܟܠܬܐ

ܡܐܡܪܐ *memra*, treatise; §10

ܡܐܢ be wearisome, *a*; §23

ܡܐܢܐ vessel, garment, possession

ܡܕܒܚܐ altar

ܡܕܝܢܬܐ city (*f.*)

ܡܕܡ something, what. ܠܐ ܡܕܡ or ܡܕܡ ܠܐ nothing

ܡܘܗܒܬܐ gift (*f.*)

ܡܘܠܟܢܐ promise

ܡܘܫܐ Moses

ܡܝܩ *pa.* mock

ܡܝܬ die; §24; *aph.* put to death

ܡܘܬܐ death (*m.*)

ܡܵܘܬ̇ܒܵܐ seat

ܡܚܐ strike, beat

ܡܚܣܒܐ at once

ܡܚܣܐ saving, life-giving

ܡܛܠ because of, on account of, concerning.

ܡܛܠ ܕ- because; §7

ܡܙܡܘܪܐ psalm

ܡܝܐ water (pl.)

ܡܝܬ pf. of ܡܘܬ

ܡܠܠ pa. ܡܲܠܸܠ speak

ܡܠܐ fill; §27

ܡܠܐܟܐ angel

ܡܠܟ aph. reign

ܡܠܟܐ king

ܡܠܟܘܬܐ kingdom (f.)

ܡܠܠ speak

ܡܠܟܬܐ queen

ܡܠܦܢܐ teacher (m.); f. ܡܠܦܢܝܬܐ

ܡܠܬܐ word (f.); pl. ܡܠܐ

ܡܢ from; §7

ܡܢ who; §4

ܡܢܐ what; §4

ܡܢܘ (= ܡܢ ܗܘ) who? §4

ܡܢܘ (= ܡܢܐ ܗܘ) what? §4

ܡܢܝܢܐ number, numeration

ܡܣܡ ܒܪܝܫܐ punishment

ܡܥܡܘܕܝܬܐ baptism (f.)

ܡܥܪܬܐ cave (f.)

ܡܦܫܩܢܐ expositor

ܡܪܐ lord, master ; abs. ܡܪܐ, cstr. ܡܪܐ

ܡܪܢ (my) lord, sir (vocative), Mar; f. ܡܪܬܝ; §10

ܡܪܝܐ the Lord

ܡܪܝܡ Mary

ܡܫܘܚܬܐ measure, age (f.)

ܡܫܚ anoint, o

ܡܫܚܐ oil

ܡܫܝܚܐ Christ, messiah

ܡܫܟܢܐ tent, tabernacle

ܡܫܡܫܢܐ minister, deacon

ܡܫܪܝܬܐ army (f.)

ܡܬܠܐ parable

ܢ nun

ܢܒܝܐ prophet

ܢܓܕ draw, e

ܢܗܘܪܐ light

ܢܘܿܢܐ fish

ܢܘܿܪܐ fire (f.)

ܢܚܬ go down, o; §20

ܢܛܪ keep, a; §20

ܢܝܣܢ April

ܢܡܘܿܣܐ law

ܢܣܒ take, a; §20

ܢܣܝܘܿܢܐ temptation

ܢܣܟ pour, o; §20

ܢܦܠ fall, e; §20

ܢܦܩ go out, o; aph. expel; §20

ܢܦܫܐ soul, self (f.); pl. ܢܦܫ̈ܬܐ

ܢܩܦ adhere, follow, a; §20

ܢܨܒܬܐ plant (f.)

ܢܩܒܐ pl. of ܐܢܬܐ

ܢܫܩ pe. (o, a), pa. kiss

ܢܬܠ impf. ܢܬܠ give; §20

ܢܬܪ wither and fall, a

ܣ semkat̲

ܣܐܒ be, grow old, a; §23

ܣܒܐ old

ܣܒܪ pe. (a), aph. think, suppose

ܣܒܪܐ hope

ܣܓܕ worship, bow down, o

ܣܓܝ (adj.) much, many; pl. ܣܓ̈ܝܐܝܢ, emph. ܣܓ̈ܝܐܐ, pl. ܣܓ̈ܝܐܬܐ, f. pl. ܣܓ̈ܝܐܬܐ.

ܣܓܝ (adv.) much, greatly

ܣܗܕ pe. (a), aph. testify

ܣܗܕܐ martyr (m.); f. ܣܗܕܬܐ

ܣܘܡ put

ܣܢܝܩܘܬܐ (n.) need

ܣܘܥܪܢܐ thing, matter

ܣܘܪܝܝܐ (adj.) Syriac

ܣܛܪ ܡܢ aside from; §11

ܣܠܩ go up; impf. ܢܣܩ; §20

ܣܡܠܐ left, left hand (f.)

ܣܢܐ hate; §26

ܣܥܪ do, perform, visit, o

ܣܦܩ be enough, a

ܣܩ imv. of ܣܠܩ

ܥ ‘e

ܥܐܕܐ festival

ܥܒܰܕ do, make, *e*; *shaph*. subjugate

ܥܰܒܕܳܐ servant, slave

ܥܒܳܕܳܐ thing, deed

ܥܒܰܪ cross, pass, transgress, *a*

ܥܓܶܠܬܳܐ heifer (*f.*)

ܥܰܕ while still. ܥܰܕ ܠܳܐ before

ܥܕܰܡܳܐ until (*prep.* +ܠ or *conj.* +ܕ)

ܥܶܕܳܢܳܐ time, moment, season

ܥܕܰܪ *pe., pa.* help

ܥܺܕܬܳܐ church (*f.*); *pl.* ܥܶܕܳܬܳܐ

ܥܺܕܬܳܢܳܝܶ ecclesiastical

ܥܽܘܕܪܳܢܳܐ help

ܥܰܘܠܳܐ wrong, injustice

ܥܰܘܳܠܳܐ iniquitous one

ܥܰܝܢܳܐ eye (*f.*), *pl. usu.* ܥܰܝܢܶܐ

ܥܺܣܽܘ Esau

ܥܰܠ enter, *o*; §25

ܥܰܠ upon, concerning, unto; §7

ܥܳܠܡܳܐ world, age. ܠܥܳܠܰܡ forever

ܥܶܠܬܳܐ reason, cause, explanation (*f.*)

ܥܰܡ with; §7

ܥܰܡܳܐ people, nation; *pl.* ܥܰܡ̈ܡܶܐ

ܥܡܰܕ *pe.* (*a*), *ethp.* be baptized; *aph.* baptize

ܥܡܰܪ dwell, *a*

ܥܢܳܐ answer

ܥܰܣܩܳܐ difficult; *f.* ܥܰܣܩܳܐ

ܥܰܦܪܳܐ dust

ܥܪܽܘܒܬܳܐ Friday

ܥܰܪܛܶܠ naked

ܥܪܰܩ flee, *o*

ܥܬܺܝܕ going to; §23

ܥܰܬܺܝܩܳܐ old

ܦ *pe*

ܦܺܐܪܳܐ fruit

ܦܰܓܪܳܐ body

ܦܽܘܡܳܐ mouth

ܦܽܘܩܕܳܢܳܐ commandment

ܦܽܘܪܩܳܢܳܐ salvation

ܦܺܝܣ persuade, ask; *ettaph.* obey; §24

ܩܛܪ bind, *o*

ܦܠܚ work, till, serve, *o*

ܦܠܚܐ soldier

ܦܢܩܝܬܐ or ܦܢܩܝܬܐ volume (*f.*)

ܦܣܣ *aph.* permit; §25

ܦܣܩ cut, cut off, *o*

ܦܪܩ *pa.* save, deliver

ܦܩܕ *pe.* (*o*), *pa.* command

ܦܪܘܩܐ saviour

ܦܪܚܬܐ bird(s) (*f.*)

ܦܪܫ separate, *o*

ܦܫܩ *pa.* expound

ܦܬܚ open, *a*

ܦܬܟܪܐ idol

ـ *ṣāde*

ܪܓܐ wish, want; *ethp.* be
    pleased, consent

ܨܒܘܬܐ thing, matter (*f.*)

ܨܒܝܢܐ wish, will

ܨܠܝ *pa.* pray; §27

ܨܠܒ crucify, *o*

ܨܠܘܬܐ prayer (*f.*); *pl.* ܨܠܘܬܐ;
    §11

ܨܥܪܐ disgrace

ܩ *qop*

ܩܐܝܢ Cain

ܩܒܠ *pa.* receive, accept;
    aph. confront

ܩܒܪ bury, *o*

ܩܕܝܫ holy

ܩܕܡ before

ܩܕܡ *pa.* do beforehand; §16

ܩܕܡܝܐ first, former; §29

ܩܕܫ *pa.* sanctify

ܩܘܝ *pa.* remain, last; §27

ܩܘܕܫܐ holiness, holy things

ܩܘܡ rise, stand; *pa.*, *aph.*
    establish; *aph.* raise
    up, set up; §24

ܩܘܪܒܢܐ offering, eucharist

ܩܘܫܬܐ truth (*m.*)

ܩܛܠ kill, *o*

ܩܛܪܓ accuse

ܩܝܡܐ covenant

ܩܠܐ voice

ܩܠܝܠ a little, a few (*indeclinable*)

ܩܢܘܡܐ person, *hypostasis*

ܩܪܐ call, read, summon; §26

ܩܪܒ draw near, touch, *o*; *pa*. offer; *aph*. fight (+ ܥܡ or ܠܘܩܒܠ)

ܩܪܒܐ battle, war

ܩܪܝܒ near

ܩܪܝܬܐ village (*f*.); §12

ܩܫܝܫܐ elder, priest

ܪ *reš*

ܪܐܙܐ mystery

ܪܒ great; *emph*., *f*. ܪܒܬܐ

ܪܒܘ ten thousand (*f*.); §29

ܪܓܠܐ foot (*f*.)

ܪܓܙ be angry, *a*; *aph*. anger

ܪܗܘܡܝܐ (*adj*.) Roman

ܪܗܛ run, *a*

ܪܘܓܙܐ anger, wrath

ܪܘܚܐ spirit, wind (*f*.); *pl*. *usu*. ܪ̈ܘܚܐ

ܪܘܚܐ ܕܩܘܕܫܐ Holy Spirit (*usu*. *m*.)

ܪܘܡ be high; *aph*. exalt; §24

ܪܚܡ love, *a*; *pa*., *ethpa*. have mercy

ܪ̈ܚܡܐ mercy (*pl*.)

ܪܚܡܐ friend (*m*.); *f*. ܪܚܡܬܐ

ܪܝܫܐ head, chief

ܪܡܐ *aph*. put, cast, throw

ܪ̈ܥܝܢܐ way of thinking

ܫ *šin*

ܫܐܕܐ demon

ܫܐܠ ask, *a*; *pa*. interrogate; *ethp*. decline (+ ܡܢ); §23; ܫܐܠ (ܒ)ܫܠܡܐ greet

ܫܒ let down, *o*; §25

ܫܒܚ *pa*. glorify

ܫܒܛ February

ܫܒܥ seven; §29

ܫܒܩ leave, dismiss, allow, forgive, *o*

ܫܒܬܐ week; sabbath; Saturday (f.)

ܫܕܪ pa. send

ܫܘܐ be equal, worthy; *pass. ptc.* ܫܘܐ equal; *aph.* make worthy; *ethp.* be made worthy

ܫܘܒܚܐ glory, praise

ܫܘܪܐ wall

ܫܝܘܠ Sheol (f.)

ܫܝܠܐ Shiloh

ܫܚܣ *see* ܐܫܟܚ

ܫܠܛ rule (+ ܒ over), *a*

ܫܠܐ be quiet, cease

ܫܠܝܐ silence. ܡܢ ܫܠܝܐ suddenly

ܫܠܝܚܐ apostle

ܫܠܝܛ lawful

ܫܠܝܡܘܢ Solomon

ܫܠܡ be finished, *a*; *pa.* finish, complete; *aph.* hand over, commit

ܫܠܡܐ peace

ܫܡܐ name; *pl.* ܫܡܗܐ or ܫܡܗܬܐ; §12

ܫܡܝܐ heaven; §12

ܫܡܝܢ heavenly

ܫܡܥ hear, *a.*; *ethp.* obey

ܫܡܫ *pa.* serve; *ethpa.* be done, take place

ܫܢܬܐ year (f.); §12

ܫܢܬܐ sleep (f.)

ܫܦܝܪ beautiful, fine; (*adv.*) well

ܫܦܪ be pleasing, *a*

ܫܩܠ take, take away, *o*

ܫܪ be proved true; *aph.* confirm, believe; §25

ܫܪܐ loose, settle, come to rest; *pa.* begin; §27

ܫܪܝܪ true. ܫܪܝܪܐܝܬ truly

ܫܪܪܐ truth

ܫܬ six; §29

ܫܬܐܣܬܐ foundation (f.); *pl.* ܫܬܐܣܐ

ܫܰܬܺܝܩ silent

ܫܬܩ be silent, o

    ܠ *taw*

ܬܰܓܳܪܐ merchant

ܬܕܝܐ breast (*m*.); §12

ܬܘܒ repent; §24

ܬܘܒ again, next. ܬܘܒ ܠܐ no longer

ܐܬܐ *see* ܐܬܐ

ܬܚܶܝܬ, -ܬܰܘܗܝ under; §7

ܬܝܳܒܘܬܐ penitence (*f*.)

ܬܠܝܬܳܝܘܬܐ Trinity (*f*.)

ܐܬܟܪܙ evangelize; §16

ܬܠܡܝܕܐ disciple

ܬܠܳܬ three; §29

ܬܶܕܡܘܪܬܐ wonder, a

ܬܡܘܙ July

ܬܰܡܳܢ there

ܬܡܳܢܝܐ eight; §29

ܬܦܐ stream

ܬܪܶܝܢ two; §29

ܬܪܝܳܢ second; §29

ܬܪܥܐ gate, door

ܬܰܪܥܝܬܐ mind, opinion (*f*.)

ܬܶܫܒܘܚܬܐ praise, hymn (*f*.); *pl*. ܬܶܫܒܚܳܬܐ

ܬܫܥ nine; §29

ܬܫܪܝ ܐܚܪܝ November

ܬܫܪܝ ܩܕܝܡ October

ܬܰܫܥܝܬܐ story, history (*f*.)

ENGLISH - SYRIAC GLOSSARY

In this glossary inflected forms are not usually given. For these, and for references to the grammar, look up the Syriac word, once found here, in the Syriac - English glossary.

A

able, be ܐܬܡܨܝ

abound ܣܓܝ

above ܠܥܠ, ܠܥܠ ܡܢ

Abraham ܐܒܪܗܡ

accept ܩܒܠ *pa.*

accompany ܠܘܝ *pa.*

according to ܐܝܟ, ܐܝܟ ܕ

accuse ܐܟܠ ܩܪܨܐ

Adam ܐܕܡ

adhere ܢܩܦ

after ܒܬܪ

afraid, be ܕܚܠ

again ܬܘܒ

against ܠܘܩܒܠ

age (*aeon*) ܥܠܡܐ

age (*of someone*) ܫܢܝܐ

alive ܚܝ

all ܟܠ- + *suffix*

allow ܫܒܩ

alone ܒܠܚܘܕ

also ܐܦ

altar ܡܕܒܚܐ

amen ܐܡܝܢ

angel ܡܠܐܟܐ

anger ܚܡܬܐ

angry, be ܪܓܙ

animals ܒܥܝܪܐ (*f.*)

anoint ܡܫܚ

another ܐܚܪܝܢ

answer ܥܢܐ

anxious, be ܝܨܦ

anything ܡܕܡ

apart from ܣܛܪ ܡܢ

apostle ܫܠܝܚܐ

appear ܚܙܝ *ethp.*

approximately ܐܝܟ

arise ܩܘܡ

army ܡܫܪܝܬܐ (*f.*)

around, go ܟܪܟ *ethp.*

as ܐܝܟ, ܐܟܘܬ-, ܐܝܟܢܐ

ashamed, be ܒܗܬ

aside from ܣܛܪ ܡܢ

ask ܫܐܠ

ask for ܒܥܐ

at ܒ-

at once ܡܚܕܐ

attack ܩܪܒ *aph.*

B

Babylon ܒܒܠ

bad, be ܒܐܫ

baptize ܥܡܕ *aph.*; be baptized, *ethp.*

baptism ܡܥܡܘܕܝܬܐ (*f.*)

basket ܐܣܦܪܝܕܐ

be ܗܘܐ

beat ܡܚܐ

beautiful ܫܦܝܪ

because ܡܛܠ ܕ

because of ܡܛܠ, ܡܛܠܬ-

become ܗܘܐ

before ܩܕܡ, ܥܕ ܠܐ

beforehand ܠܩܘܕܡ; do beforehand ܩܕܡ *pa.*

beget ܝܠܕ *aph.*

begin ܫܪܐ *pa.*

behind ܒܣܬܪ

behold! ܗܐ

believe ܗܝܡܢ

beloved ܚܒܝܒ

below, beneath ܬܚܝܬ-, ܬܚܬ, ܡܢ ܠܬܚܬ

beside ܓܢܒ

between ܒܝܢܬ, ܒܝܬ, ܒܝܢܝ

bind ܐܣܪ, ܦܟܪ

bird(s) ܦܪܚܬܐ

bishop ܐܦܝܣܩܘܦܐ

blaspheme ܓܕܦ *pa.*

blasphemy ܓܘܕܦܐ

bless ܒܪܟ *pa.*

blessed one ܛܘܒܢܐ (*m.*), ܛܘܒܢܝܬܐ (*f.*)

blessing ܒܘܪܟܬܐ (*f.*)

blood ܕܡܐ

body ܦܓܪܐ, ܓܘܫܡܐ

bone ܓܰܪܡܐ

book ܟܬܳܒܐ

born, be ܝܠܕ *ethp.*

bread ܠܰܚܡܐ

breast ܬܕܳܐ

bring ܐܝܬܝ *aph.*, ܡܛܐ *aph.*

brother ܐܰܚܐ

build ܒܢܐ

burn ܝܩܕ *intransitive;*
  transitive aph.

bury ܩܒܪ

but ܐܠܐ, ܕܝܢ

buy ܙܒܢ

by - ܒ, ܡܢ, ܠܘܬ

C

Cain ܩܐܝܢ

call ܩܪܐ

can *see* able

care, take ܝܗܒ *ethp.*, ܝܨܦ

carry ܡܛܐ *aph.*

cast ܪܡܐ *aph.*

cause ܥܠܬܐ (f.)

cave ܡܥܰܪܬܐ (f.)

cease ܫܠܐ

change (*v. trans.*) ܚܠܦ
  shaph.

chief ܪܫܐ

child ܝܠܕܐ (*m.*), ܛܠܝܐ
  (f.)

childhood ܛܠܝܘܬܐ (f.)

choose ܓܒܐ

Christ ܡܫܝܚܐ

Christian (*adj.*) ܟܪܣܛܝܢܐ

church ܥܕܬܐ (f.)

city ܡܕܝܢܬܐ (f.)

cleave ܢܩܦ

cling ܢܩܦ

close ܐܚܕ

clothe ܠܒܫ *aph.*

clothing ܠܒܘܫܐ

coin ܙܘܙܐ

come ܐܬܐ

come down ܢܚܬ

command ܦܩܕ *pe.*, *pa.*

commandment ܦܘܩܕܢܐ

commit ܣܥܪ *aph.*

companion ܚܒܪܐ (*m.*)
  ܚܒܪܬܐ (f.)

compare ܚܣܡ *pa.*

compassion, have ܪܚܡ
   pa., ethpa.

compel ܐܠܨ / *pe., pa.*

concerning ܡܛܠ

confess ܝܕܐ *aph.*

confirm ܫܪ *aph.*

confront ܚܕ *aph.*

confuse ܕܠܚ *palpel*
   ܕܠܚܕܠ

consent ܨܒܐ *ethp.*

consume ܐܟܠ

convict ܚܣܕ *pa.*

correct, be ܬܪܨ

counsel ܡܠܟܐ

covenant ܩܝܡܐ

cover ܚܣܐ *pa.*

create ܒܪܐ

creator ܒܪܘܝܐ

cross (n.) ܨܠܝܒܐ

cross (v.) ܥܒܪ

crowd ܟܢܫܐ

crown ܟܠܝܠܐ

crowned, be ܟܠܠ *ethpa.*

crucify ܨܠܒ

cultivate ܦܠܚ

curse (v.) ܠܘܛ

cut, cut off ܦܣܩ

D

daughter ܒܪܬܐ (*f.*)

David ܕܘܝܕ

day ܝܘܡܐ

deacon ܡܫܡܫܢܐ

death ܡܘܬܐ (*m.*)

debt ܚܘܒܐ

decline ܨܠܐ *ethp.*

deed ܥܒܕܐ

delay ܫܘܚܪ / *aph.*

deliver (set free) ܦܪܩ *pa.*;
   (hand over) ܡܫܠܡ *aph.*

demon ܫܐܕܐ

destroy ܐܒܕ / *aph.*

die ܡܝܬ (*pf.* ܡܝܬ)

difficult ܥܣܩ

disciple ܬܠܡܝܕܐ (*m.*),
   ܬܠܡܝܕܬܐ (*f.*)

disgrace ܨܥܪܐ

dismiss ܫܒܩ

displeasing, be ܟܐܫ

dispute ܫܢܢܬܐ

do ܥܒܕ, ܕܒܪ

doctrine ܡܠܦܢܘܬܐ

donkey ܚܡܪܐ (m.), ܐܬܢܐ (f.)

door ܬܪܥܐ

down, go ܢܚܬ

draw ܢܓܕ

draw near ܩܪܒ

dressed, be ܠܒܫ

dust ܥܦܪܐ

dwell ܥܡܪ, ܫܪܐ

E

ear ܐܕܢܐ (f.)

earth ܐܪܥܐ (f.)

eat ܐܟܠ

ecclesiastical ܥܕܬܢܝܐ

Eden ܥܕܢ

eight ܬܡܢܝܐ

elder ܩܫܝܫܐ

emissary ܐܝܙܓܕܐ

emperor ܡܠܟܐ

encourage ܠܒܒ pa.

endure ܣܝܒܪ pay'el ܣܝܒܪ

enemy ܒܥܠܕܒܒܐ

enter ܥܠ

enough, be ܣܦܩ

Ephrem ܐܦܪܝܡ

equal ܫܘܐ

equal, be ܫܘܐ

especially ܝܬܝܪܐܝܬ

establish ܩܘܡ pa., aph.

eternity ܥܠܡܐ

eucharist ܩܘܪܒܢܐ

evangelize ܣܒܪ aph.

Eve ܚܘܐ

even (adv.) ܐܦ

every ܟܠ

everyone ܟܠܐܢܫ

everything ܟܠܡܕܡ

evil ܒܝܫܐ

evil, be ܟܐܫ

evil, do ܒܐܫ aph.

Evil One, the ܒܝܫܐ

exalt ܪܡ aph.

exceed ܝܬܪ ܡܢ

expel ܢܦܩ aph.

explanation ܬܽܠܓܳܐ (*f.*)
expound ܦܫܶܩ *pa.*
eye ܥܰܝܢܳܐ (*f.*)

F

face ܐܰܦܶܐ (*f. pl.*)
fair ܫܰܦܺܝܪ
faith ܗܰܝܡܳܢܽܘܬܳܐ (*f.*)
far be it! ܚܳܣ
fall ܢܦܰܠ
fashion (*v.*) ܓܒܰܠ
fate ܚܶܠܩܳܐ
father ܐܰܒܳܐ
favour (*n.*) ܛܰܝܒܽܘܬܳܐ
fear (*v.*) ܕܚܶܠ
fear (*n.*) ܕܶܚܠܬܳܐ (*f.*)
fearsome ܕܚܺܝܠ
festival ܥܐܕܳܐ
few, a ܩܰܠܺܝܠ
field ܚܰܩܠܳܐ (*f.*)
fight ܩܪܶܒ *aph.*
fill ܡܠܳܐ
find ܐܶܫܟܰܚ
fine ܫܰܦܺܝܪ
finished, be ܫܠܶܡ
fire ܢܽܘܪܳܐ (*f.*)
first (*adj.*) ܩܰܕܡܳܝ;
(*adv.*) ܠܽܘܩܕܰܡ
fish ܢܽܘܢܳܐ
fitting, is ܘܳܠܶܐ
five ܚܰܡܶܫ
flesh ܒܶܣܪܳܐ
flee ܥܪܰܩ
follow ܢܩܶܦ
food ܡܶܐܟ݂ܽܘܠܬܳܐ (*f.*)
foot ܪܶܓܠܳܐ (*f.*)
for (*conj.*) ܓܶܝܪ
for (*prep.*) ܠ-
force (*n.*) ܚܰܝܠܳܐ
forgive ܫܒܰܩ
form (*v.*) ܓܒܰܠ
fortress ܚܶܣܢܬܳܐ (*f.*)
foundation ܫܶܬܐܣܬܳܐ (*f.*)
four ܐܰܪܒܰܥ
friend ܪܳܚܡܳܐ (*m.*), ܪܳܚܡܬܳܐ (*f.*)
from ܡܶܢ
fruit ܦܺܐܪܳܐ

G

gain ܢܟܘ

garden ܓܢܬܐ (f.)

garment ܠܒܘܫܐ, ܡܐܢܐ

gate ܐܪܥܐ

Genesis ܒܪܝܬܐ

gift ܡܘܗܒܬܐ (f.)

give ܝܗܒ, impf. ܢܬܠ

give birth to ܝܠܕ

glad, be ܚܕܝ

glorify ܫܒܚ pa.

glory ܐܝܩܪܐ, ܬܫܒܘܚܬܐ (f.)

go ܐܙܠ

go down ܢܚܬ

go out ܢܦܩ

go up ܣܠܩ

God ܐܠܗܐ

going to ܥܬܝܕ

gold ܕܗܒܐ

good ܛܒ

good, be ܛܐܒ

good, do ܛܐܒ aph.

gospel ܐܘܢܓܠܝܘܢ

governor ܗܓܡܘܢܐ

grace ܛܝܒܘܬܐ (f.)

great ܪܒ

Greek (adj.) ܝܘܢܝ

greet ܫܐܠ (ܒ)ܫܠܡܐ

groan ܬܢܚܬܐ (f.)

ground ܐܪܥܐ (f.)

guard ܢܛܪ; ܗܘܐ ethp.

guilty ܚܝܒ

H

hand ܐܝܕܐ (f.)

hand over ܐܫܠܡ aph.

hasten ܣܘܚ saph'el ܐܣܬܘܚ

hate ܣܢܐ

he ܗܘ

head ܪܫܐ

hear ܫܡܥ

heart ܠܒܐ

heat ܫܚܢܐ (f.)

heaven ܫܡܝܐ

help (v.) ܥܕܪ pe., pa.

help (n.) ܥܘܕܪܢܐ

here ܗܪܟܐ

heretic ܗܪܛܝܩܐ

hide ܚܡܐ *pa.*

high, be ܪܘܡ

history ܐܷܚܢܝܬܐ (*f.*)

hold ܐܚܒܝ ܒ-

holiness ܩܲܕܝܫܘܬܐ (*f.*),
ܡܩܲܕܫܐ

holy ܩܲܕܝܫ

Holy Spirit ܪܘܚܐ ܘܡܩܲܕܫܐ
(*usu. m.*)

honour (*v.*) ܝܩܲܪ *pa.*

honour (*n.*) ܐܝܩܵܪܐ

hope (*n.*) ܣܲܒܪܐ

house ܒܲܝܬܐ (*m.*)

how ܐܲܝܟܲܢܐ, ܐܲܝܡܸܟ

how much, many ܟܡܐ

however ܕܝܢ

human (*adj.*) ܐܢܫܝ

hundred ܡܐܐ

hymn ܐܘܡܚܦܣܝܬܐ (*f.*)

I

I ܐܸܢܐ, ܐܢܐ

idol ܦܬܲܟܪܐ

if ܐܢ, ܐܠܘ

---

ill ܟܪܝܗ

ill, be ܟܪܗ *ethp.*

immediately ܡܚܣܐ

in ܒ-

indebted ܚܲܝܒ

inform ܝܕܥ *aph.*

inherit ܝܪܬ

injustice ܥܲܘܠܐ

inside (*n.*) ܓܲܘܐ; (*adv.,
prep.*) ܠܓܲܘ (ܡܢ)

instead of ܚܠܦ

interrogate ܫܐܠ *pa.*

Israel ܐܝܣܪܐܝܠ

J

Jacob, James ܝܲܥܩܘܒ

Jerusalem ܐܘܪܫܠܡ

Jesus ܝܫܘܥ

Jew ܝܗܘܕܝܐ, ܝܗܘܕܝܐ

John ܝܘܚܢܢ

joy ܚܲܕܘܬܐ (*f.*)

Judas ܝܗܘܕܐ

judge (*v.*) ܕܢ

judge (*n.*) ܕܲܝܢܐ

judgement ܕܝܢܐ
Judith ܝܗܘܕܝܬ
June ܚܙܝܪܢ
just (*adj.*) ܟܐܢ; justly ܟܐܢܐܝܬ
justice ܟܐܢܘܬܐ (*f.*)

K

keep ܢܛܪ
kill ܩܛܠ
kind (*n.*) ܙܢܐ
king ܡܠܟܐ
kingdom ܡܠܟܘܬܐ
kiss ܢܫܩ *pe.*, *pa.*
know ܝܕܥ

L

lady (*title*) ܡܪܬܝ
lamb ܐܡܪܐ
land ܐܪܥܐ (*f.*)
language ܠܫܢܐ
last ܐܚܪܝ
last (*v.*) ܩܘܐ *pa.*
law ܢܡܘܣܐ
lawful ܫܠܝܛ
lay ܣܘܡ
lead (*v.*) ܕܒܪ
leader ܡܕܒܪܢܐ
learn ܝܠܦ
leave ܫܒܩ
left (hand) ܣܡܠܐ (*f.*)
lest ܕܠܡܐ, ܕܠܐ
let down ܫܒ
letter ܐܓܪܬܐ
life ܚܝܐ (*pl.*)
life-giving ܡܚܝܢ
lift up ܪܘܡ *aph.*
light ܢܘܗܪܐ
like (*prep.*) ܐܝܟ, ܐܟܘܬ-
like, be ܕܡܐ
liken ܕܡܐ *aph.*
likeness ܕܡܘܬܐ (*f.*)
listen to ܫܡܥ
little ܩܠܝܠ
live (*v.*) ܚܝܐ
living ܚܝ
look (at) (ܒ-) ܚܘܪ
loose (*v.*) ܫܪܐ, ܫܒܩ

lord مُدَا

Lord, the مُدَنِا

lose احب / aph.

lost, be أُحَب

love (v.) سحا، وْشِع / aph.

love (n.) سفَحُا

M

make محب

make known سِلا aph.

man جَحدَا

many هَنيهاب

martyr هُدوها (m.);
هُدوها (f.)

master وَخُا، مُدَا

Mary مَدنَم

matter رحفَمُا، هِفَحدَنُا (f.)

measure محهَسجُا (f.)

meat خُهدَا

memra مَامِدَا

merchant أَيخُا

mercy وَنْفحُا

mercy, show وْسِع، مَّع pa.,
ethpa.

messiah محفحُا

mighty work عَملُا

mind أُوحدَهُا (f.)

moment خِدَا

monastery وَمِنُا (f.)

monk وَمِنُا

month مَنسُا

more (than) مَاحَن (مَّن)

Moses مُهَهُا

mother أُمُا (f.)

mountain طَفَوُا

mourn احلا / ethp.

mouth فَهمُا

move (v. trans.) ہوا aph.

movement مَهحُا

much مَنيُا

mystery أَوَازُا

N

naked حَنيَلحَب

name محمُا

nation مَحمُا

nature مَنُا

near مَنيَد

need ܣܘܢܩܢܐ
new ܚܕܬܐ, *f.* ܚܕܬܐ
news ܛܒܐ
next ܬܘܒ, ܦ
night ܠܠܝܐ (*f.*)
nine ܬܫܥ
no ܠܐ
no longer ܠܐ ܬܘܒ, ܬܘܒ ܠܐ
not ܠܐ, ܠܘ
not, there is ܠܝܬ
nothing ܠܐ ܡܕܡ
now ܗܫܐ
number, numeration ܡܢܝܢܐ

O

o! ܐܘ, ܐܘ
obey ܫܡܥ *ethp.*
of ܕ-
offer ܩܪܒ *pa.*
offering ܩܘܪܒܢܐ
oil ܡܫܚܐ
old ܥܬܝܩ, ܩܫܝܫ
old, be or grow ܣܐܒ
on ܥܠ
on behalf of ܚܠܦ
one ܚܕ
open (*v.*) ܦܬܚ
opinion ܬܪܥܝܬܐ (*f.*)
or ܐܘ
other ܐܚܪܝܢ
outside (ܡܢ) ܠܒܪ
owe ܚܘܒ

P

palace ܗܝܟܠܐ; ܒܝܪܬܐ (*f.*)
parable ܡܬܠܐ
peace ܫܠܡܐ
penitence ܬܝܒܘܬܐ (*f.*)
people ܥܡܐ; ܐܢܫܐ, ܒܢܝ ܐܢܫܐ
perform ܣܥܪ
perhaps ܕܠܡܐ
perish ܐܒܕ
permit ܦܣ *aph.*
person ܒܪ ܐܢܫܐ
person (of the Trinity) ܩܢܘܡܐ
petition ܒܥܘܬܐ (*f.*)

place اُوَثَا, وَثَحِبَا, اُوَثَحِبَا (f.)

plant (v.) بَرَث

plant (n.) نُوِرحَبَا (f.)

pleasing, be حفَ

pleased, be رِحا ethp.

plunder حَر

pour لحَم

pour out اُحَّم

power حَبِلَا

praise مقَحسَا,
        اَحِحفسَخَا (f.)

pray بلي pa.

prayer رِلخفَأَا

preach هزا aph.

preserve نَحَّ

press احي / pe., pa.

price لَبتَخَا

priest حَمِحَا, حُهبَا

prison حَسِه اَهَبتَزَا

promise (v.) محلحم

promise (n.) محَلحفبَا

prophet نحَبَا

psalm محَاهفوَأ

punishment محَحم حزَبحَا

pure وَحبَا, f. وَحفَا

pure, be وِحَ or وِحفَا

purify وحا pa.

put محَم, وَمحا صهمحا aph.

Q

queen محَلحمِا (f.)

quiet, be محَك

R

raise محَم aph., زَمحم aph.,
        مصحلحم aph.

read مزَا

reason نَحلحِبَا (f.)

receive محلا pa.

reckon سمَحَ

refuse حاللا ethp.

reign محلحم aph.

rejoice سحبا

rejoicing (n.) صَبةَمَأَا (f.)

remain محَا pa.

remain over نَحَوَ

repent لاهحَ

reprove حمَم aph.

require ܚܫܚ

return ܗܦܟ

reveal ܓܠܐ

right ܐܘܢ

right (hand) ܝܲܡܝܼܢܵܐ (f.)

righteous ܐܘܢ, ܟܹܐܢ

righteousness ܐܘܡܝܘܬܐ (f.)

rise ܩܘܡ

rise (of the sun) ܕܢܚ

river ܢܗܪܐ

road ܐܘܪܚܐ / (f.)

robber ܓܢܣܝܐ

Rome ܪܗܘܡܐ

Roman (adj.) ܪܗܘܡܝܐ

roof ܐܓܪܐ

run ܪܗܛ

S

sabbath ܫܒܬܐ

sacrifice (v.) ܕܒܚ pe., pa.

sacrifice (n.) ܕܒܚܐ (f.)

saint ܩܕܝܫܐ (m.); ܩܕܝܫܬܐ (f.)

sake of, for the ܡܛܠ

salvation ܦܘܪܩܢܐ, ܚܝܐ

sanctify ܩܕܫ pa.

save ܣܡ aph., ܦܪܩ

saving ܡܦܪܩ

saviour ܦܪܘܩܐ

say ܐܡܪ

sea ܝܡܐ

see ܚܙܐ

seed ܙܪܥܐ

seek ܚܫܚ

seize ܐܚܕ -ܕ

self ܢܦܫܐ (f.)

sell ܙܒܢ pa.

send ܫܕܪ pa.

separate (v.) ܦܪܫ

servant ܥܒܕܐ

serve ܫܡܫ pa., ܦܠܚ

service ܬܫܡܫܬܐ (f.)

set ܣܘܡ

set up ܩܘܡ aph.

settle ܝܬܒ

seven ܫܒܥܐ

shake (intransitive) ܙܘܥ;
(transitive) aph.

she ܗܺܝ

shed (*blood*) ܐܶܫܰܕ

Sheol ܫܺܝܘܠ

show ܚܰܘܺܝ *pa.*

shut ܐܶܚܰܕ

sick ܟܪܺܝܗ

sick, be ܟܪܰܗ *ethp.*

side ܓܰܒܳܐ

silent ܫܰܬܺܝܩ

silent, be ܫܬܶܩ

sin (*n.*) ܚܛܺܝܬܳܐ (*f. no pl.*),
ܣܰܟܠܘܳܬܐ

sing ܙܡܰܪ *pe., pa.*

sir ܡܳܪܝ

sister ܚܳܬܐ

sit ܝܺܬܶܒ

six ܫܬܐ

sleep ܫܶܢܬܐ (*f.*)

slightly ܩܰܠܺܝܠ

small ܙܥܘܪ

Solomon ܫܠܶܝܡܘܢ

soldier ܦܳܠܚܐ, ܐܶܣܛܪܰܛܺܝܘܳܛܐ

someone ܐ̱ܢܳܫ

something ܡܶܕܶܡ

son ܒܪܐ

soul ܢܰܦܫܐ (*f.*)

speak ܡܰܠܶܠ *pa.* ܡܠܐ

speech ܡܰܡܠܠܐ

spirit ܪܘܚܐ (*f.*); *see also*
    Holy Spirit

stand ܩܳܡ

stay ܩܰܘܺܝ *pa.*

stone (*n.*) ܟܺܐܦܐ (*f.*)

story ܐܶܫܬܰܥܺܝܬܐ (*f.*)

stranger ܐܟܣܢܝܐ

strength ܚܰܝܠܐ

strengthen ܚܰܝܶܠ *pa.*

stretch out ܦܫܰܛ *aph.*

strong ܚܰܣܺܝܢ

subjugate ܫܰܥܒܶܕ *shaph.*

suppose ܣܒܰܪ *pe., aph.*

suckle ܝܰܢܶܩ *aph.*

suddenly ܡܶܢ ܫܶܠܝܐ

suffice ܣܰܦܶܩ

suffer ܚܰܫ

sun ܫܶܡܫܐ

synagogue ܟܢܘܫܬܐ (*f.*)

Syriac (*adj.*) ܣܘܪܝܳܝܐ,
    (*n.*) ܣܘܪܝܳܝܘܬܐ

T

take ܡܩܠܐ, ܢܣܒ

take place ܗܘܐ *ethpa.*

taste (*v.*) ܛܥܡ

teach ܐܠܦ

teacher ܡܠܦܢܐ (*m.*),
ܡܠܦܢܝܬܐ (*f.*)

teaching ܡܠܦܢܘ, ܡܠܦܢܘܬܐ

tear (*of the eye*) ܕܡܥܬܐ (*f.*)

tell ܐܡܪ, ܡܠܠ *aph.*

temple ܗܝܟܠܐ

temptation ܢܣܝܘܢܐ

ten ܥܣܪ

ten thousand ܪܒܘ (*f.*)

tent ܡܫܟܢܐ

testify ܣܗܕ *pe., aph.*

thank ܝܕܐ *aph.*

that ܗܘ (*m.*), ܗܝ (*f.*)

that (*conj.*) ܕ-

then ܗܝܕܝܢ, ܗܟܝܠ

there ܐܡܢ

there is ܐܝܬ

there is not ܠܝܬ

therefore ܡܛܠܗܢܐ ܗܟܝܠ

these ܗܠܝܢ

they ܐܢܘܢ, ܗܢܘܢ (*m.*); ܗܢܝܢ, ܐܢܝܢ (*f.*)

thing ܚܕܐ, ܚܕܐܝܬ (*f.*), ܡܕܥܡ

think ܣܒܪ; ܚܫܒ *pe., aph.*

this ܗܢܐ (*m.*), ܗܕܐ (*f.*)

those ܗܢܘܢ (*m.*), ܗܢܝܢ (*f.*)

thousand ܐܠܦ

three ܬܠܬܐ

throw ܪܡܐ *aph.*

thus ܗܟܢܐ

till (*v.*) ܦܠܚ

time ܙܒܢܐ, ܥܕܢܐ

to -ܠ, ܠܘܬ

today ܝܘܡܢܐ

tomb ܩܒܪܐ

touch ܓܫ

towards ܠܘܬ

transgress ܥܒܪ

transmit ܫܠܡ *pa.*

tree ܐܝܠܢܐ

Trinity ܬܠܝܬܝܘܬܐ (*f.*)

true ܫܪܝܪ

true, be proved ܫܪ

truth ܩܘܫܬܐ, ܩܘܫܬܐ (m.)

two ܬܪܝܢ (m.), ܬܪܬܝܢ (f.)

U

under ܬܚܝܬ, ܬܚܘܬ-

unless ܐܠܐ

until ܥܕܡܐ (+ ܠ- or ܘ-)

upon ܥܠ

V

vessel ܡܐܢܐ

village ܩܪܝܬܐ, pl. ܩܘܪܝܐ (f.)

vineyard ܟܪܡܐ

vision ܚܙܘܐ

voice ܩܠܐ

W

wail ܝܠܠ aph.

wages ܐܓܪܐ

walk ܗܠܟ pa.

wall ܐܣܬܐ

want ܒܥܐ

war ܩܪܒܐ

water ܡܝܐ (pl.)

way ܐܘܪܚܐ (f.)

way of life ܕܘܒܪܐ (pl.)

we ܚܢܢ, ܚܢܢ

wearisome, be ܠܐܐ

week ܫܒܘܥܐ (f.)

well (adv.) ܫܦܝܪ

well (in health) ܚܠܝܡ

well, be made ܚܠܡ ethp.

what ܡܢܐ, ܡܐ, ܡܘܢ, ܡܢܐ

when ܐܡܬܝ (ܘ-); ܡܐ ܘ-; ܟܕ (-ܘ)

where ܐܝܟܐ

which ܐܝܢܐ (m.), ܐܝܕܐ (f.), ܐܝܠܝܢ (pl.)

while ܟܕ, ܟܡܐ

white ܚܘܪ

who ܡܢ

whole ܟܠ- + suffix

why ܠܡܢܐ

widow ܐܪܡܠܬܐ (f.)

wife ܐܢܬܬܐ (f.)

will (n.) ܨܒܝܢܐ

wind ܪܘܚܐ (f.)

wisdom ܚܟܡܬܐ (f.)

wise ܚܟܝܡ

wish (v.) ܪܰܓ

wish (n.) ܪܶܓܬܐ

with -ܥܲ, ܥܰܡ

within (ܓܰܘ) ܠܓܰܘ

without ܕܠܐ

witness, bear ܣܗܶܕ pe.,
   aph.

woe ܘܳܝ

woman ܐܰܢ̱ܬܬܐ (f.)

womb ܟܰܪܣܐ (f.)

wonder ܬܶܗܪܐ

word ܡܶܠܬܐ (f.)

work ܦܠܰܚ

world ܥܳܠܡܐ

worship (v.) ܣܓܶܕ

worthy, be ܫܘܳܐ

wrath ܪܘܓܙܐ

wretched ܕܳܘܶܐ

write ܟܬܰܒ

wrong (n.) ܥܰܘܠܐ

Y

year ܫܰܢ̱ܬܐ

you sing. ܐܰܢ̱ܬ (m.), ܐܰܢ̱ܬܝ
   (f.); pl. ܐܰܢ̱ܬܘܢ (m.),
   ܐܰܢ̱ܬܶܝܢ (f.)